YOUNG PEOPLE'S SOCIAL ATTITUDES

Having Their Say — The Views of 12–19 Year Olds

Edited by
HELEN ROBERTS AND DARSHAN SACHDEV

First published in 1996 by Barnardo's
Tanners Lane
Barkingside
Ilford
Essex
IG6 1QG

Charity Registration No. 216250

A catalogue record for this book is available from the British Library.

ISBN 0 902046 30 6

YOUNG PEOPLE'S

Contents

Acknowledgements

Barnardo's first acknowledgement must be to the children and young people who so wholeheartedly participated in the first *Young People's Social Attitudes Survey*. As will become apparent in the course of the report, there were very few non-responses or 'don't knows' from the children and young people who freely gave their time for this piece of work. We hope that offering them a public voice in this way will serve as a 'thank you' and will provide a positive reply to the question so many survey respondents ask (or ask themselves), 'will it be of any use?'

Two distinguished authors joined the Barnardo's team who wrote this report, and we are grateful for their willingness to do so. Ann Oakley, Director of the Social Science Research Unit and Professor of Sociology and Social Policy at the University of London Institute of Education, has written the chapter Gender Matters: Man the Hunter; David Walker, a broadcaster and journalist specializing in social affairs, has written on Young People, the Media and Politics. The editors also wish to acknowledge the assistance they have had from Barnardo's library, and from our Publications Officer, Ravi Wickremasinghe.

In working on the *Young People's Social Attitudes Survey* with colleagues at Social and Community Planning Research, we are grateful for the warm collaboration of Lindsay Brook, Roger Jowell and in particular Alison Park, as well as SCPR colleagues in data processing, data analysis, and interviewer training. We find it difficult to believe that we would have obtained the quality of data described below without the experience and enthusiasm of SCPR's interviewers.

A number of chapters in this report have benefited from the data on adult respondents from the British Social Attitudes survey and the merged adult and young people's dataset from the two 1994 surveys, and we are grateful to SCPR for giving us access to this material.

Barnardo's is happy to acknowledge all of these parties, and we look forward to seeing more detailed analyses of the data collected, now that these will be, along with the British Social Attitudes data, in the public domain and available from the ESRC's data archive.

Preface

Much of the systematic information about children in our society is factual. It relates mainly to family circumstances, health, education and socio-economic situations. Much of it derives from routine data sources, administrative returns, censuses and large-scale surveys. Answers are usually provided by parents, teachers or other adults. In recent years, methods of collecting data from children themselves have been developing. Much progress has been made in charting aspects of children's behaviour such as smoking and drinking. Such information can only be obtained by surveying samples of children using methods appropriate to their age and assuring them that their answers will be treated with complete confidentiality. Now these methods have been extended a stage further — to the description and analysis of children's attitudes.

When the *British Social Attitudes Survey* began in 1983 there was some scepticism about the value of a survey principally about attitudes. But the huge series of data now accumulated provides a unique view of British life to use in conjunction with the mass of "factual" information about people's lives. It allows us to compare people in different age, sex and social groups, to study the relationships of attitudes in different spheres and, most importantly, to monitor changes over time.

This book marks the potential beginning of a similar accretion of attitude data about children and young people. The first analysis is presented here. The potential for other work on the survey data and for comparisons with the adult data is large; the possibility of future rounds of the survey is exciting.

KAREN DUNNELL
Office of Population Censuses and Surveys

Foreword

The measure of a society's civilization can be judged by the way in which it treats its children. In the UK, many indices of children and young people give grounds for optimism. Children in the UK grow up to live longer than they did a century ago (though not as long as in a number of other industrialized countries); perinatal and infant mortality have fallen (but not as steeply as in some other parts of Europe) and, for many, the standard of living has risen.

As a recent Barnardo's report has shown, most children today are materially better off than their parents were at the same age. They enjoy more pocket money, toys and treats. Yet the sheer speed with which society has changed over the last 30 years is a source of unease. Parents may worry that although their own families are thriving, a substantial minority of families have had little or no share in the economic growth of the past 15 years (Barnardo's, 1995:15).

How are children and young people themselves responding to this changing climate? Children do not have a vote, but they do have a voice. Barnardo's work to improve the lives of children, young people and their families living in greatest need goes alongside a commitment to speaking out for young people or enabling them to speak out for themselves. In the UK in general, we have been remarkably reluctant to work directly with children and young people to find out more about the worlds they inhabit, or would like to inhabit. Our aim, in co-operating with SCPR in producing this first survey of young people's social attitudes to sit alongside the main *British Social Attitudes Survey*, is to provide a benchmark for looking at the changing attitudes of children and young people; to look at their adherence (or otherwise) to 'traditional' values, and the differences, if any, between adults and children in social attitudes.

The UN Convention on the Rights of the Child, to which the UK is a signatory, is an aspiration statement, focusing on protection, provision and participation for children. An absolute minimum in terms of the participation of children and young people is for us to listen to them, and respect their worth as individuals. To know what children think about schooling and education, family life, crime and punishment, and to know about their attitudes to right and wrong is a first step in including children and young people in the social order. Giving them the opportunity to reflect on some of these issues is an important part of children's moral and spiritual education.

There has recently been talk of the dangerous alienation of young people who are, according to reports of a recent study of 18–34 year-olds (Wilkinson and Mulgan, 1995), disaffected and resentful. This is not (or not yet) reflected in the attitudes of the 12–19 age group reported here. Although there is some scepticism towards the political process, the responses of these young people give us cause to feel that we may have a generation of young people who are rather more tolerant, honest and committed to principles of sound education, stable family life, and welfare than they are credited with. They may indeed be more committed to these things than we deserve in a climate where so many are facing uncertain futures — a labour market without jobs, a society where probity in public life has come under scrutiny, and where spending on state welfare falls well below that of a number of other European countries.

I commend this work to you, and the approach it embodies, of taking the views of children and young people seriously. We very much hope that this will be the first in a series of reports which will enable us to look at trend data on children and young people, and compare it with adults in the same household. Barnardo's is pleased to have been instrumental in initiating this work, and we hope that those with a policy interest in children and young people will take the opportunity to make this survey a regular event.

MICHAEL JARMAN
Director of Childcare
Barnardo's

References

Barnardo's (1995), *The Facts of Life*, Barkingside: Barnardo's.

Wilkinson, H. and Mulgan, G. (1995), *Freedom's Children. Work, relationships and politics for 18–34 year olds in Britain today*, Paper No 17, London: Demos.

Notes on contributors

Mike Hughes is a Principal Officer, Research and Development at Barnardo's. He has previously worked as a teacher, social work practitioner and manager and social researcher. His research interests include the social consequences of facial disfigurement (doctoral thesis), the use of information technology in social welfare, community development and anti-poverty work, and education (particularly behaviour management in education). He is particularly concerned with Barnardo's in north-east England and Scotland. His publications include: *The Social Consequences of Facial Disfigurement* (in press); numerous papers on the impact of child care services in Barnardo's; *School's Out* (with Ruth Cohen, Laura Ashworth and Maud Blair), a study of exclusion from school; and articles (with Shani Fancett) on information technology in social welfare. His special focus is the development of an anti-poverty strategy for Barnardo's.

Eva Lloyd joined Barnardo's in 1995 as a Principal Officer, Research and Development with special responsibility for work with families with young children. For the last 10 years she has been engaged in social policy research concerning children, first as a psychologist member of multidisciplinary research teams at the Thomas Coram Research Unit, University of London, and later for Save the Children UK. Her work includes co-editing *Motherhood: Meanings, Practices and Ideologies* (with Ann Phoenix and Anne Woollett) and writing *Baby Language* (with Maire Messenger Davies and Andreas Scheffler). Among her other publications are several on prisoners' children, including *Prisoners' Children: Research, Policy and Practice*.

Diana McNeish is a Principal Officer, Research and Development at Barnardo's. She worked as a practitioner and manager in Social Services before joining Barnardo's. She has a particular research interest in disadvantaged young people and has written a number of Barnardo's publications on the impact of social policy on children and families including *Liquid Gold — the cost of water in the nineties* and *Poor Deal — the cost of living in the nineties*. She was co-author of *Doing Time — the impact of temporary accommodation on children* and *Playing it Safe — today's children at play*. She is currently also a part-time lecturer in Child Welfare and Youth Justice at the University of Leeds.

Tony Newman has worked for Barnardo's as Principal Officer, Research and Development, since 1989. He began a career in social work in 1975, working with Indo-Chinese refugees in the USA at the end of the war in Vietnam. He developed an interest in research during a lengthy career with the Cardiff-based NIMROD service, the UK's first comprehensive community-based provision for people with learning disabilities and their families. Still based in South Wales, he has lectured at Cardiff University and Cardiff Institute of Higher Education. Recent publications include a study of credit unions in *Critical Social Policy* and Barnardo's studies on family centres, young people with cystic fibrosis and partnership with people who use services. He is currently completing a study on colleges of further education which has been carried out with a team of young disabled people.

Ann Oakley is Director of the Social Science Research Unit and Professor of Sociology and Social Policy at the University of London Institute of Education. She has been carrying out research in the area of women's health and the family for many years, and has a particular interest in combining quantitative and qualitative research methods. Her books include: *The Sociology of Housework, Women Confined, Subject Woman, The Captured Womb, and Social Support and Motherhood.* She has a strong research interest in the development of systematic reviews, and the evidence basis of welfare services. She has done some joint work with Barnardo's on this, funded by the ESRC.

Alison Park is a Senior Researcher at Social Community Planning Research, and a Co-director of the *British Social Attitudes Survey* series. She is also involved with the British Election Panel Study and the International Social Survey Programme. Her research interests include politics, the attitudes of young people, employment and training. Most recently, she has written on young people and politics (in *British Social Attitudes: the 12th Report*).

Helen Roberts is Co-ordinator of Research and Development at Barnardo's, and Honorary Senior Fellow with the Social Statistics Research Unit, City University, London. Her most recent book is *Children at Risk? Safety as a Social Value* (with Susan J. Smith and Carol Bryce). She has written on research methodologies, and the health of women and children. Her work includes the edited collections *Social Researching: Politics, Problems, Practice* (with Colin Bell), *Doing Feminist Research, Women's Health Counts* and *Women's Health Matters*. Her current preoccupation is the evidence basis for child welfare interventions.

Darshan Sachdev joined Barnardo's as a Senior Research Officer in 1995. Before joining Barnardo's, she researched into the unmet needs of Asian elderly people in the areas of social services, health services and welfare benefits provision. She has eight years' experience of working with minority ethnic communities. In early 1993, she completed her PhD which explored the effects of psychocultural factors on the socialization of Indian and indigenous British children living in England. Her research interests include cross-cultural research, educational research and attitude surveys.

David Walker is a journalist specializing in social and public policy. Until recently, he was Urban Affairs Correspondent of the BBC, and used to present Radio Four's Analysis programme. Before that, he worked for *The Economist* and then *The Times* as leader writer and social policy correspondent. He is a member of the advisory panel of the Centre for the Study of Electoral and Social Trends and Centre for Housing and Urban Research and a Trustee of the Public Finance Foundation. As a Harkness Fellow in the USA from 1977 to 1979 he worked in the US Congress. His books include *Media Made in California*, *Sources Close to the Prime Minister* and *The Times Guide to the New British State*. He is currently completing a book on the future of the public service ethos and acting as rapporteur of the Joseph Rowntree Foundation inquiry into the future of central and local government relations.

Introduction

When the first volume in SCPR's *British Social Attitudes* (BSA) series was published, Sir Claus Moser, former head of the Government Statistical Service welcomed an initiative that would enable civil servants, academics, journalists and others to explore how we think and feel as a nation. That first survey, and the eleven which have followed, have tracked social attitudes via representative samples of adults living in Britain, and have provided one means by which we can begin to understand the way our beliefs, attitudes and values change over time. A strength of the BSA survey is precisely that it is a series: the data become more useful over time, providing a regular, systematic and rigorous means of measuring and monitoring changes in British public attitudes. From the start, the survey has tracked the views of adults aged 18 or over. But what do we know of the attitudes of younger adults and children?

In 1993, Barnardo's approached Social and Community Planning Research with a proposal for a survey to explore the social attitudes of a group of children and young people which would be comparable to the adult survey in terms of quality and substantive subject matter. Barnardo's interest in this stemmed from our commitment to listening to young people and speaking out on their behalf or enabling them to speak out themselves. Barnardo's works with those in greatest need, but in order to understand the lives and values of those at the margins of society, we need to have access to the wider picture. What does a representative sample of young people think about crime and punishment, education, family life, racism or equal opportunities? Are young people disaffected? It has been pointed out by others that the 'youth question' is a fertile source of imagery of a turbulent, even apocalyptic, character and that youthful deviance and dissent have been seen as portents of serious eruptions of intergenerational conflict. This conception co-exists with less publicized studies, indicating mass adolescent conformity to core values and beliefs (Downes and Rock, 1990). A *Young People's Social Attitudes Survey* provides an opportunity to look over time at these core attitudes and beliefs, and to compare these to the attitudes and beliefs of adults.

As with the early BSA reports, our aim in this book has been to provide a publication that describes and discusses the data, rather than providing those detailed statistical analyses which, now that the data are in the public domain, we hope and expect a variety of scholars and others will carry out. We very much hope that this will be the first in a series, so that the attitudes of young people may be explored once every two or three years, producing the valuable trend data which has been so important to our understanding of social attitudes since the inception of the adult study. The continuation of this study will depend on outside financial support, and we are confident that potential funders will see the value of a regular, and high-quality, source of data on the views of children and young people over time.

This book provides a first look at the principal findings of the *Young People's Social Attitudes* (YPSA) *Survey*. The theme underlying each chapter is how the data 'fit' (or otherwise) with other key findings in the area under discussion and what some of the findings are from this study. Running through the book is a discussion of the salience of these data for those of us for whom an understanding of the marginalization and exclusion of young people — whether through income, geography, unemployment, crime or ethnicity — is a major concern.

Ex cathedra statements on the young are commonplace, and there have been a number of *ad hoc* studies and regular reports, such as the Walls pocket money survey (Bird's Eye Walls, 1995), which have given a snapshot of family life in Britain or of the views of young people. Furnham and Gunter's *Anatomy of Adolescence* (1989), based on a sample of National Association of Youth Club members interviewed during 1985 as part of International Youth Year, is a classic, and is referred to by a number of contributors to this report. But we have lacked the foundations for a regular, authoritative survey of the views and attitudes of young people, demonstrating the direction of any changes in social attitudes among young people. We know quite a lot about what adults think of young people and how that has changed over time. But how do young people think adults are doing? What are their views of right and wrong? What basic political knowledge do they have? What are their views on education, on the relationship between different ethnic groups or on gender inequalities? As others have pointed out, if we want to know about what people think of their world and themselves, there is no substitute for asking them (Turner and Martin, 1981).

While market researchers have not been slow to understand the importance of listening to children, government, academic and research institute researchers have been less inclined to work directly with young people — a caution which may have a basis in important methodological, ethical and other concerns, some of which Barnardo's has recently explored (Alderson, 1995). The issue of whether children can be reliable respondents sits alongside the question of whether they should be. Are they able to participate in an informed way in research? Alderson's (1993, 1995) work suggests that they are, and that we have a great deal to learn from them.

We were relieved to find that this first YPSA survey demonstrates that children and young people are both willing and able to respond in a thoughtful way to an attitude survey. If they are willing to give their views on subjects on which they are, in a sense, 'experts', such as family life and education, we (that is 'we' in the broadest sense, including politicians, government departments, service providers and others) should be willing to listen to what they have to say, and incorporate their views into our understanding of what it is to be a child or young person. Without asking children and young people for their views directly, it is all too easy to impute views to them, and to stereotype 'youth' on the basis of small samples or anecdotes.

It should be emphasized here, as Roger Jowell explained in respect of adults in his introduction to the first BSA survey, that no finding we report can be taken as a precise statement about young people's social attitudes in Britain. As Jowell wrote: "Every finding is an approximation, part of a body of evidence which needs to be examined in the context of other evidence." (Jowell, 1984:7) Alongside quantitative social surveys such as YPSA, there is a place for careful qualitative research, teasing out the meanings that children and young people attach to what they are saying, and exploring how they come to hold the beliefs, values and attitudes that they do. But as the chapters in this report show, reliable data of the kind produced by YPSA provide a fruitful basis for informed discussion of what it is to be a young person in Britain today.

The survey

Appendix I gives details of the sample and the methods used, and Appendix II reproduces the questionnaire, with the percentage distribution of responses in full. The reader may, however, find it helpful at this stage to have some basic background information about the survey.

British Social Attitudes is an annual nationwide survey that started in 1983. In 1994, some 3469 people aged 18 and over were interviewed. In the same year, for the first time, the survey was supplemented by the YPSA survey. All young people aged 12–19 who lived in the same household as a British Social Attitudes respondent were eligible for interview. Of the 735 eligible young people, some 580 (79% of eligible respondents) were interviewed. Given BSA's sample size, and hence that of the YPSA survey, the number of minority ethnic respondents is low. One would normally exclude from analysis numbers as small as these, but it would be ironic in the extreme to exclude from this report precisely one of those groups facing routine exclusion in the UK today. All our descriptions of these data are simply that, and our speculations subject to further work with larger samples. With SCPR, we intend to look at ways of augmenting this aspect of the survey in future surveys.

The questions were subject to piloting, and we had some useful feedback from the interviewers involved in the pilot: "It's the easiest pilot I've done — they wanted to take part,"; "It's good that children are being asked,"; and "I couldn't believe the way they responded. It was brilliant." Interviewers felt that the association of the survey with Barnardo's made their task easier — families recognized the charity. One series of questions on the age at which children and young people should be expected to carry out household tasks such as washing-up, or making their own beds resulted in some interesting comments. Interviewers discerned from the pilots a tendency of children to give an age one year older than they actually were. Other responses included (for washing-up), "when you can reach the sink." One interviewer reported a child saying that the age at which children should be expected to help with these tasks was, "when I grow up." The interviewer said, "I gave her a look to see if she was taking the mick, and she said, 'No, I mean it. I'm a child. I'm going to have to do it for the rest of my life.'" The feedback we had from the pilot made it clear not just that children and young people could answer the questions, but that they found it fun and liked being asked.

About half the questions in the YPSA survey were also asked of adults in one of the versions of the BSA survey. This means that the answers given by young people to these questions can be compared with those given by adults in general, or adults in the same household. Some of these data are described in this volume but, on the whole, we hope that the detailed exploration of these data will be an opportunity grasped by other researchers. The remaining questions were unique to the YPSA survey. Although we do not (or do not yet) have trend data on young people, in some cases, we have been able to compare the responses of the children and young people interviewed to responses given in earlier years by adult respondents.

Topics covered in the YPSA survey were as follows:

- 'Age of consent'
- Judgements of right and wrong
- Education, school life and sex education
- Fear and experience of crime
- Crime and punishment
- Gender roles and family life

- Racial prejudice and discrimination
- Political knowledge, political interest and party identity
- Important factors in 'doing well in life'
- Life ambitions and aspirations

The chapters that follow do not present a picture of disaffected and rebellious youth. As Tony Newman points out in the first chapter, although the notion that 'young people like things pretty much the way that they are' would be unlikely to produce a successful newspaper headline, the overall picture of young people portrayed by these data do not suggest that children and young people are storming the bastions of adult power. They want parents to have a bigger say than them in the educational curriculum, they feel that drug use at school should be punished, they don't believe people should get married while very young, or leave school too early, or have sex below the current age of consent, and almost a third support current film censorship laws.

The survey confirms the general indifference of this age group to party politics. David Walker, in this report, and Alison Park (1995) in the 12th BSA report explore this issue, with Walker discussing the proposition that there is a minimum base of knowledge necessary for effective participation in the political process. If children and young people are to be (or are) citizens, this is a key question.

But childhood and youth are not simply a preparation for adulthood and much of the strength of the data collected rest on the unique picture they help us construct of the social attitudes of young people who are so frequently judged on the basis of sketch and stereotype.

References

Alderson, P. (1993), *Children's consent to surgery*, Buckingham: Open University Press.

Alderson, P. (1995), *Listening to Children: Children, ethics and social research*, Barkingside: Barnardo's.

Bird's Eye Walls (1995), *The Walls Monitor*, 1995, London.

Downes, D. and Rock, P. (1990), 'Preface' in Davis, J., *Youth and the Condition of Britain, Images of Adolescent Conflict*, London: The Athlone Press.

Furnham, A. and Gunter, B. (1989), *The Anatomy of Adolescence: Young People's Social Attitudes in Britain*, London: Routledge.

Jowell, R. (1984), 'Introducing the Survey', in Jowell, R. and Airey, C. *British Social Attitudes, the 1984 Report*, Aldershot: Gower.

Park, A. (1995), 'Teenagers and their Politics', in Jowell, R., Curtice, J., Park, A., Brook, L. and Ahrendt, D. (eds), *British Social Attitudes: The 12th report*, Aldershot: Dartmouth.

Turner, C.F. and Martin, E. (1981) (eds), *Surveys of subjective phenomena: a summary report*, Washington, DC: National Academy Press.

1 Rights, rites and responsibilities: the age of transition to the adult world

TONY NEWMAN

Whatever the method adopted, whether the young are disciplined, lectured, consciously fought, permitted to run wild or even antagonised by the adult world — the result is the same. The little Manus become the big Manus, the little Indian the big Indian.

(Mead, 1977: 195–6)

In this matter of transition from child role to adult role our society is, again, quite deviant compared to other societies.

(Stephens, 1963: 385)

Children and very elderly people are commonly the subject of a similar enquiry: 'How old are you?' A query that for much of our life span may be considered impertinent at best, carries both legitimacy and meaning when addressed to either of these two constituencies. The precision of children's answers is an indication of the centrality of age to their sense of self. It has been argued (James and Prout, 1990: 222), that age is one of the key features in understanding how we construct the notion of childhood: "... concepts of age are the main scaffolding around which western conceptions of childhood are built and it is through reference to concepts of age that the daily life experiences of children are produced and controlled."

The chronological sequence of infancy, childhood, adolescence, adulthood, middle age and old age is embedded in popular understanding as an inevitable outcome of human biology. 'You aren't old enough yet', 'you're too old for that', 'when you're older'; these phrases and their variations are part of our collective memories and we repeat them to our own children. 'Childhood' is presented and internalized by us as less a state of being than a state of becoming, an apprenticeship where each feeling, thought and action becomes a preparation for childhood's goal — adult maturity. Since the publication of Aries' work on the history of childhood (Aries, 1962), the notion of childhood as a social construct, rather than a biological condition, has dominated sociological discourse. Only in this century, it is suggested, has there emerged 'the idea of childhood as a discrete period of life in which the physical, mental and emotional patterns of an adult are developed and strengthened' (Jones and McNeely, 1981: 13). Feminist and post-modernist critiques, particularly in the context of child sexual abuse, have dwelt on the 'silence' of children (Glaser and Frosh, 1988; Gittins, 1993; Alderson, 1995) and have drawn parallels with the historical silence of other oppressed groups. That children should be seen and not heard is more than a cliché of Victorian parental discipline. Historically, children have had nothing to say that could not be said better by adults. The concept of childhood as a prison, with adults as warders, has led to the same dialectical tools being used to dissect the anatomy of children's oppression as have been used to address the issues of race, class and gender. The distribution of power in child/adult relationships is, according to this paradigm, as imbalanced as that in male/female, black/white, abled/disabled, first world/third world, gay/straight relationships and should be analysed within the same political framework. Childhood, the argument proceeds, is therefore constructed through the medium of adult-centric assumptions, and the empowerment of children can only be achieved through the deconstruction of this model.

The nature of childhood

The notion of childhood as, at least in part, a social construct is largely uncontentious. The parameters of childhood — as defined by the age of majority — are shifted periodically and have been so moved several times within the recent past. Childhood, as defined by these age-related criteria, has been both lengthened (education, sex, working) and shortened (voting, marrying). At present, children are held responsible for their actions at 10, can own an air rifle at 14, may leave school, buy cigarettes, work full-time and have sex with a heterosexual partner at 16, join the armed forces at 17, and purchase alcohol and vote at 18. It has been suggested (Freeman, 1983: 7) that there is no logic in these distinctions and this view is supported by the considerable variation in age limits that exists in different western countries. Age-related privileges are rooted in the first modern wave of children's rights advocates, the nineteenth century social reformers who sought better treatment and conditions for child labourers. The elimination of these chronological distinctions has been seen, particularly by the 'second generation' of children's rights advocates (Holt, 1975; Neill, 1976; Farson, 1979; Hoyles, 1979; Franklin, 1986) as the cornerstone of children's liberation. The reluctance of children to embrace this ideology was typically rationalized by the application of a Marxist analysis: children have internalized their own oppression and are unable to transcend this position without an external stimulus to awaken their dormant revolutionary consciousness. As Firestone (1972: 101–2) proposed:

> *"We must include the oppression of children in any program of feminist revolution or we will be subject to the same failing of which we have so often accused men ... of having missed an important substation of oppression merely because it didn't directly concern us."*

The necessary response to this analysis was succinctly summarized by Holt (1975: 15), who suggested that:

> *"... the rights, privileges, duties, responsibilities of adult citizens be made* *available* [author's emphasis] *to any young person, of whatever age, who wants to make use of them."*

The third generation of children's rights advocates, which has been described as 'pragmatist' (Lindsay, 1992), has sought to negotiate a middle ground between those who believe children's rights can be best defended by age-related gateposts and the protection of adults and those who see any attempt by adults to define children's best interests as patriarchal and self-serving. This 'middle way' characterizes the stance of most children's rights organizations today, which accept the premise that, as Freeman (1983: 4) asserts, 'interference with a child's liberty is an inescapable consequence of the biological and psychological dependence of children'. The acceptance of a child's dependence on the adult world leads to the inevitable corollary: childhood and adulthood are separate domains and children, in some way and by some means, must pass from one to the other. The issue, for adults and children, is how this transition is to be managed and what balance must be struck between control and autonomy.

Age, rights and responsibilities

Age-related empowerment remains problematic. A commitment by adults to nurture the growing child's critical faculties, extending and stretching his or her capacity to reach independent decisions sits uneasily with the crude finality of a legal age limit. The UN Convention on the Rights of the Child, adopted in 1989 (and ratified, with some reservations, by the UK in 1991), sites the child's locus of independence and autonomy in his or her level of maturity and present decision-making capacity (Articles 5 and 14). However, despite extensive theoretical expositions of the development of childhood autonomy (Piaget, 1928; Maslow, 1970; Erikson 1977), it is generally accepted that no widely accepted model for assessing the capacity of children to make such decisions currently exists (Hart, 1991: 56).

Parents, and indeed children, are routinely confronted with the practical problem of age-related autonomy. Is Judy sufficiently mature to look after the baby while we slip out for a drink? Is Usha old enough to stay out until ten o'clock tonight? Surely Karen and David are far too young to have a serious relationship? Although it may be of little comfort to ordinary citizens to be told that the finest developmental psychologists of the twentieth century have yet to come up with a definitive answer to such queries, the age-related data from the *Young People's Social Attitudes Survey* does illuminate how young people themselves respond to some of these questions.

The table on the next page illustrates the ages at which young people believe that they can or should undertake various activities. The rows show the most frequently mentioned age (mode) and average age (median) for each question, respectively. The data show a hierarchy of age-related milestones, progressing from making one's own bed and helping with the washing-up at around 10 years, to marriage and voting at 18 years. The gradient appears logical when seen from this perspective. Smaller tasks and lesser degrees of autonomy are built on in an incremental pattern, culminating with two rites of passage that cement a young person's place as part of the civic unit: marriage and the power to influence the decision-making processes of society.

Most responses mirror existing legislation — a phenomenon common in adult surveys — though interestingly, young people want fewer rights than the state already extends to them in relation to marriage. Conservatism rather than a radical desire to overthrow adult dominion is the overall message of the data, with only minor domestic tasks being seen as legitimate tasks for under-fourteens.

We can also see from the data that the young people interviewed largely accept the notion of age-related rights. An overwhelming number of responses to questions about activities mediated by legislation locate the preferred age of majority between the ages of 16 and 18. In doing so, young people appear to acquiesce in the widely accepted adult premise that certain activities should be forbidden to children until a particular age has been attained, although some disparity may exist as to what this age should actually be. A very small number of young people — all very low single-figure percentages — replied 'at any age' or 'when ready' to questions in this part of the survey — an option not offered as a response, and thus only used when someone gave the answer of his or her own accord. This implies a rejection

Age-related milestones

	Age most commonly cited (mode)	Average age (median)
At what age do you think people should be expected to ...		
...make their own bed	10 (22%)	10
...do washing-up	10 (24%)	10
At what age do you think people should be allowed to ...		
...be left alone for the evening	14 (24%)	14
...get a part-time job	14 (27%)	15
...babysit a child of 5	16 (28%)	15
...leave school	16 (67%)	16
...have sex	16 (54%)	16
...leave home	16 (46%)	17
...drive a car	17 (36%)	17
...see any film in the cinema	18 (29%)	16
...buy alcohol	18 (45%)	18
...vote in a general election	18 (56%)	18
...marry	18 (44%)	18

of the liberationist position of early proponents of children's rights, which suggested that the denial to children of almost all rights enjoyed by adults constituted an act of oppression similar to that experienced by other social groups. Children, it appears, still recognize their vulnerability and feel the need to be protected from certain activities (or not be expected to undertake them) until a particular age has been reached.

Age

The notion of an age-related transition from the domain of childhood to the domain of adulthood is supported by the profile of the data when examined by age bands, as shown in the table.

Age-related milestones by age band of respondent

	Age bands (years)		
	12–15	**16–17**	**18–19**
% of young people in three age bands (12–15, 16–17 and 18–19) who selected 16, 17 and 18 years as the age when they should be allowed to…			
vote			
16 years	38	14	9
17 years	6	3	1
18 years	41	77	80
leave home			
16 years	49	47	34
17 years	12	12	3
18 years	23	25	43
marry			
16 years	22	22	15
17 years	9	8	5
18 years	39	49	55
buy alcohol			
16 years	32	29	12
17 years	17	14	8
18 years	36	53	69

The pattern is quite clear. Younger children want adult responsibilities at a younger age. Older children are already beginning to assume adult perspectives. Although 28% of all children identified 16 as the preferred age for voting rights, this response was given by 38% of the 12–15 age band but by only 9% of children in the 18–19 age band. Similarly, although the preferred legal age of leaving home was given by 49% of 12–15-year-olds as 16 years and 23% as 18 years, these figures were reversed for 18–19-year-olds, with 34% identifying 16 and 43% citing 18 years. This general trend is marked, though varying in magnitude, throughout the survey, with the widest age-related variation occurring in the above examples and the least in relation to the age of sexual activity, watching any film in the cinema and leaving school.

Age, then, is clearly a variable that affects the opinions of young people, though whether the probable congruence of the 18–19 age band with adult opinions reflects a mature consideration of the consequences of adult behaviour or a jealous attempt to guard hard-earned privileges is a matter of conjecture.

Gender

Gender, on the other hand, appears less significant. It will not come as a surprise to parents to learn that more boys (27%) than girls (20%) wish to drive cars at 16 years, nor that only 25% of boys felt that under-tens should help with the washing-up compared with 37% of girls. Bed-making evoked a similar lack of male enthusiasm, with 42% of boys considering it an appropriate task for under-tens, in contrast to 56% of girls.

Forty-six per cent of girls and 41% of boys believed that the legal age of marriage should be 18, and only 19% of girls and 24% of boys 16 years. Boys were rather more confident at being left alone for the evening: 22% felt this was appropriate between the ages of 8 and 12, compared with 17% of girls. However, extreme gender differences were notable by their absence. The differences that were observed were far smaller than the age-related variations. It is difficult to speculate, in the absence of any previous data, whether this parity is recent, and if so, whether any movement is as a result of a change in male or female beliefs, or both.

Race

Race appeared to have a certain amount of influence on some aspects of young people's opinions, though, again, a minor one in comparison with age. However, the variation that was detected was quite marked. The figures should be treated with caution, given the small numbers of non-white respondents (*n*=38). Of the 'racial' categories used (Black, Asian, White), only the Asian category included enough non-White respondents (*n*=32) to justify any analysis. In relation to leaving home, 56% (18) of young Asian people selected the age of 18, compared with 25% of white respondents. Forty-one per cent (13) of young Asian people opted for 18 years as the age at which children should be allowed to have sex; this age was chosen by only 11% of Whites. Figures for those who cited the age of 16 years were 22% (7) and 56%, respectively. Marriage at 16 was a right supported by 22% of Whites, but only 12% (4) of Asians.

Asian young people (37% (12)) were twice as likely as white young people to choose the ages of 16 to 19 as the minimum age to be left alone for the evening.

This would appear to present a picture of young Asian youth as wedded to a more 'traditional' morality and family structure, which indeed may be the case. However, as we only have limited information about the Asian groups represented, it is too easy to fall into the trap of clutching at stereotypes. No variation of similar magnitude was apparent between racial groups in other questions.

Class and family structure

The data were also examined for variation on the basis of class and family structure. Categories for the latter included one-parent families, reconstituted families and two-parent families, and a small number of young people living independently. Hypothesized differences, relating to greater levels of independence in one-parent families, did not emerge; in fact, little or no significant variation was noted in any category in this part of the survey. Class, on the other hand, did appear to play a part. The congruence of opinions between the children of professional/managerial and intermediate non-manual classes and those of semi-skilled and unskilled manual workers on the age for starting work reflects, perhaps, a recognition by working-class children of the reality of the job market. Middle-class children, as one would expect, were more likely to cite an older age for leaving school (21% post-16) than working-class children (9% post-16). Similarly, only 9% of middle-class children chose under-16 options, compared with 19% of working-class children. However, the largest variation was in the area of domestic responsibilities, with only 17% of working-class children believing washing-up was a task that should be expected of under-tens, compared with 32% of middle-class children. Making beds appeared to be even more attractive as a task to middle-class children: 58% thought this should be done by under-tens. Working-class parents may, sadly, expect the co-operation of only 28% of their offspring in bedmaking. (Parents, however, may justifiably wish to draw the attention of researchers towards the tenuous link between evinced attitudes and subsequent behaviour in the performance of both these activities.)

Legal age limits

The survey did not test children's knowledge about the correct legal ages at which certain activities could be undertaken. A recent survey (Brown, 1992) examined this issue, and revealed that 73% of their sample (*n*=739) knew the correct voting age, 68% the minimum age to drive a car, 80% buying alcohol, 56% the age of marriage and 94% the age of leaving school. The most frequent incorrect answer related to the minimum age for having part-time employment, where only 10% gave the correct response.

As we are unable to distinguish, in our survey, between the responses of young people who knew minimum legal ages and those who did not, we are unable to explore to what extent this knowledge influenced the replies. In relation to the age of part-time work, young people were actually (and uniquely, in relation to the questions asked) less likely to cite a younger age than the legal minimum. Seventy-three per cent of responses were spread fairly evenly across the 14–16 age range. Similarly, 69% of responses to the question on what age should a young person be able to babysit a child of five occurred in the 14–16 year band. Neither finding illustrates an over-eager desire to assume adult responsibilities.

Sex education

The table below illustrates the relative power young people believe should be exercised, by parents and children, on the issue of sex education in schools. Young people were asked whether all children aged 11 and under should have sex education at school, or whether their parents should be allowed to choose. The same question was asked about children aged 12–16 years.

Sex education in schools

	Sex education should be:	
	Compulsory	**Parents' choice**
	%	%
for all children aged 11 and under	37	61
for all children aged 12–16	53	9

Opinions on sex education in schools show a clear demarcation between the degree of parental influence before and after the age of 11 years. Almost two-thirds of young people (61%) felt this should be the parents' choice before the age of 11. In addition to the 37% who believed that under 11s should have sex education, 53% of children believed that all 12–16-year-olds should receive sex education. Although we do not have the opinions of younger children on this matter (and the opinions of teenagers may be influenced by a desire to put clear blue water between themselves and their former lives as juniors and infants), the reliance on parents' judgement before 11 years would not appear to support more radical advocates of compulsory early childhood sex education.

Influence on curricula content and punishments used in schools

The tables below compare the power that young people believe should be exercised by children and by parents on the issues of punishments and curricula content.

Influence on what is taught in school

	How much say should children have in what is taught in schools?	How much say should parents have in what is taught in schools?
	%	%
All	7	7
Quite a bit	27	39
Some	41	47
Not very much	17	5
No say at all	8	2

Influence on what punishments are used in school

	How much say should children have in the kinds of punishments that are used in schools?	How much say should parents have in the kinds of punishments that are used in schools?
	%	%
All	7	18
Quite a bit	18	36
Some	35	31
Not very much	23	9
No say at all	15	5

When asked what influence children should have over what is taught in schools and how children are punished, the total responses for 'some of the say' and 'quite a bit of the say' were 68% and 53%, respectively. Parental influence over these issues was held to be even more important, however, with totals for the same categories being 86% and 68%. More working-class children believed that they and their parents should have all of the say in what is taught in schools (15% and 10% respectively) than middle-class children (5% and 4%). Young people, it seems, appear to value parental opinion in relation to these issues. Unfortunately, we have no information on what degree of influence the respondents (or their parents) had in reality over either issue and thus it is hard to know to what extent respondents were considering a theoretical experience. However, the results show a desire on the part of children for both themselves and their parents to make a real contribution to aspects of school life that previous generations may have felt (or been told) were the exclusive reserve of professionals.

Interestingly, variation by race was also noted in relation to the degree of influence young people should have over what is taught in schools, with 59% (19) of Asian children choosing the options 'all of the say' or 'quite a bit of the say' compared with 32% of white children. Similarly, a greater degree of influence was preferred by Asian children in the matter of punishment, with figures of 50% (16) and 24%, respectively, for the above categories of response. Opinions of parents' optimum degree of influence, however, was similar in all racial categories.

Drugs

The use of drugs at school brings a punitive reaction from young people, with 55% believing that expulsion is the preferred response. The response of boys and girls is equally punitive, though slightly more girls (32%) than boys (26%) are prepared to explore options that do not include suspension or expulsion. Nineteen per cent of young people believed that 'a lot' of students had drugs at school, but 29% had no knowledge of students using drugs. The largest percentage, 47%, believed it happened 'a little'. As one might expect, knowledge of drug use at school increased with age, with just under one-third of 18–19-year-olds (32%) believing that 'a lot' of students at their school had drugs at school.

Young people's beliefs

The overall picture of young people portrayed by these data supports the hypothesis that the levels of responsibility demanded by young people may not be as radical as some commentators have believed to be the case. Children and young people are not yet storming the bastions of adult power. They want parents to have a bigger say than themselves in the educational curriculum, they feel that drug use at school should be punished severely, they don't believe people should get married at a young age, leave school too early or have sex below the current age of consent, and almost a third support current film censorship laws. A sizable proportion of respondents — usually around a quarter — wish for certain rights at the age of 16 rather than 18 years (voting, buying alcohol), not in themselves issues that constitute a major social revolution. The desire for some rights may be theoretical rather than actual — one may reasonably speculate as to how many of the 46% of the respondents who believed children should have the right to leave home at 16 actually will. Although 'young people like things pretty much the way they are' as a newspaper headline would be unlikely to move many copies, it is a view supported by similar recent surveys. Furnham and Gunter (1989: 192), in a review of four surveys of adolescent attitudes conducted in the 1980s, concluded that:

> *"Young people seem to be involved in both 'youth culture and adult culture', seeking neither to subvert the latter nor replace it with the former. That is not to say they are against change, but rather the change they appear to favour is moderate and limited."*

Rights, rites and responsibilities

We have no information, from the raw data, on how young people interpret the meaning of the activities that seal their entry to the adult world. Are voting, having sex, working, getting married and being free of age-related censorship civil rights that should be granted on the basis of natural justice at a particular age? Does acquisition of these rights imply any concomitant responsibilities, and if so, to whom or what? Holt's (1975) manifesto mixes, without comment, rights and privileges with duties and responsibilities. The former are rarely refused, the latter are, often. The former are associated with liberty and freedom; they are universal, cannot be abrogated and are often linked with the term 'inalienable'. Duties and responsibilities, conversely, are wearisome — we are intoxicated by the notion of an inalienable right, burdened by the notion of an inalienable responsibility. Rights are defended by poets and revolutionaries, responsibilities by pedagogues and retired colonels. The relationship between these two concepts is central to the alchemical change whereby a girl becomes a woman and a boy a man. Most religious traditions involve the inheritance of both rights and responsibilities, in both private and public ceremonies at particular ages, though the age at which spiritual, as opposed to secular, duties are assumed may not always coincide. Within, for example, the Jewish tradition, a boy enters the adult world at the age of 13, a girl at 12. This brings the privileges of maturity but also demands of the child obedience to the law of Moses. Rights, within most ancient traditions (Van Gennep, 1960), are counterbalanced by concomitant responsibilities. This balance is a delicate one, as Gluckman (1962: 29) comments:

> *"The social order is so impregnated with moral judgements that it can be disturbed by any failure to fulfil an obligation."*

Ritual, it has been suggested, and not necessity, is the mother of invention. In a collection of essays on the future of the family written over two decades ago (Miller, 1970: 32), Miller predicted that:

> *"... society will probably make conscious and unconscious attempts to re-create tribal society at the same time as psychological disintegration increases."*

Lacking, or having lost, the capacity to celebrate the passage of children to new phases of life through ritual, age-defined parameters have become the medium whereby we enact our tribal customs. Despite their apparent (and actual) arbitrary nature, it is difficult to conceive of another mechanism through which the secular rites that now mark the passage from childhood to adulthood can be commonly understood and maintained. The protection of children and the defence of their rights is not just a result of modern sensitivities, it is also the result of expediency. A century ago, the majority of the labouring classes in every country in Europe was employed in agriculture (Hobsbawm, 1994), a massively — at that time — labour-intensive industry. The work of children was essential in order that the urban masses could sleep with full bellies. We may be repelled by the often brutal and unrewarded lives of rural Victorian children, but then we rarely go to bed hungry. Children in earlier times, "... were indispensable for the survival of the family unit. Working in fields and shops they built a life and a nation." (Brendtro *et al.*, 1990: 28). The simplistic notion that childhood is a modern 'invention', conceived in response to the needs of an economy moving from feudalism to capitalism, has been largely dispelled by more recent studies of European cultural history (McLaughlin, 1976; Pollock, 1983; Wilson, 1984). The suggestion that childhood, as a concept, did not exist in the Middle Ages (Firestone, 1971) is simply wrong. Children in medieval Europe were not, as in the Roman *familia*, considered *patria potestas*; contemporary sources refer to parental responsibilities in ways little different to the late twentieth century (Shahar, 1992: 13):

> *"Theologians, preachers and authors of didactic works enlarged on the duties of parents towards the children entrusted to them for safekeeping; it was incumbent on them to support them, protect them, raise them properly, and give them a Christian education. They were responsible for their children before God."*

While childhood, it is clear, has no 'natural' configuration, it is at least in part what the adult world or the civic unit wishes, or more correctly, needs it to be. However, both children and adults are part of the same human ecology and their respective roles are conditioned by something more atavistic than an abstract commitment to social justice. No longer needed to gather the harvest or support aged parents in the absence of a welfare state, children have, by any economic analysis, changed in the space of a few generations from an asset to a liability. As Macfarlane (1986: 72) observed:

> *"... in the domestic mode of production, where resources are pooled between the generations and parents and children form one economic and social unit of consumption and production, each parental generation benefits from children."*

Their function may be expressed in macro-economic terms, as any middle-aged person wondering who will be paying for state pensions in the twenty-first century will know, but their function in the micro-economy of the family is wholly one of negative equity. With the growing irrelevance of the millennia old motivations for producing children, lineage (too patriarchal) and labour supply (unnecessary), the concentration of social science on the aetiology of rights has rather begged the question, 'what are children for?'

The optimum balance between rights and responsibilities, which has been the focus of much recent discussion (Etzioni, 1993; Selbourne, 1994), is hardly a new debate for parents, few of whom have not completed the sentence, 'if you're old enough to … you're old enough to…'. The preoccupation of social scientists with deconstructing the social meaning of childhood may be less important to the welfare of children and their families than the emergence of a new consensus on not just the rights children should have, but when and how they should become adults, and how this transition should be marked.

The agonized debates of the last few decades over the respective roles of parents and children may well be a necessary corrective to a defunct and damaging paternalism. The crumbling of the post-industrial revolution demarcation lines between adulthood and childhood, which have been a feature of the last 30 years, have brought obvious benefits to children. The stripping of the veil from the horrors of child sexual abuse, the legitimation of children's voices, the breaking down of social and occupational barriers that entrapped girls have been long overdue transformations. However, one feature of young people's responses in this survey is the weight placed on parents' opinions. The genesis of the children's rights movement in the western world followed hard on the explosion of youth culture in the 1960s and the growing disgust with the conduct of an immoral war in Indo-China. 'Never', children were told, 'trust anyone over 30'. 'We are', graffiti in London read, 'the writing on your wall'. Anomie and alienation are not conditions that solely affect young people; adults, and especially parents, have also been inevitably unbalanced by the shifting sands of social change.

The role of adulthood, and especially parenthood, implies the possession of greater wisdom than that of children. 'When a father helps a son', the proverb goes, 'both laugh. When a son helps a father, both cry.' The emotional integrity of parents depends in part on their being able to offer guidance to their children. It may thus come as some comfort to parents to know that, from this sample at least, young people still see themselves as being different from adults and in need of parental help. The most striking aspect of these data exhibit the changing perspective of children on ages of responsibility over a narrow age band, illustrating that young people do not view themselves as a homogenous group, with similar rights and privileges. The ancient and basic premise — that adult status is acquired primarily by the passage of time and that certain responsibilities, rights and individual autonomy should be granted at particular chronological stages — is largely accepted, although some dispute may exist about exactly what these ages should be. The importance of age should not surprise us, as anyone who has observed (or remembered) the disdain with which children may treat former peers who by virtue of being born a few months earlier have not yet attained a particular age-related milestone will know.

In the midst of the intense debate provoked by the emergence of the 'counter-culture' in the 1960s, Keniston (1971: 399) observed:

> *"... as the youthful opposition ceases to be youthful, it must constantly guard against further evolution into a reactionary force."*

On the evidence of these data, the kind of intra-group consciousness necessary to underpin the dialectic of oppression, which has been applied by some commentators to the position of children, appears to be little more than wishful thinking. Children may be children first; they are also not children for very long.

References

Alderson, P. (1995), *Listening to Children: Children, Ethics and Social Research*, Barkingside: Barnardo's.
Aries, P. (1962), *Centuries of Childhood*, London: Jonathan Cape.
Brendtro, L., Brokenleg, M. and Van Bockern, S. (1990), *Reclaiming Youth at Risk: Our Hope for the Future*, Bloomington, Indiana: National Educational Service.
Brown, I. (1992), *The Criminal Justice System: Schoolchildren Speak Out*, Huddersfield: Kirklees Criminal Justice Inter-Agency Forum.
Erikson, E. (1977), *Children and Society*, St Albans: Paladin.
Etzioni, A. (1993), *The Spirit of Community: Rights, Responsibilities and the Communitarian Agenda*, New York: Crown Publishing Group.
Farson, R. (1979), *Birthrights*, Harmondsworth: Penguin.
Firestone, S. (1972), *The Dialectic of Sex*, London: Paladin.
Franklin, R. (1986) (ed.), *The Rights of Children*, Oxford: Blackwell.
Freeman, M.D.A. (1983), *Rights and Wrongs of Children*, London: Francis Pinter.
Furnham, A. and Gunter, B. (1989), *The Anatomy of Adolescence: Young People's Social Attitudes in Britain*, London: Routledge.
Gittins, D. (1993), *The Family In Question*, (2nd edn), Basingstoke: Macmillan.
Glaser, D. and Frosh, S. (1988), *Child Sexual Abuse*, Basingstoke: Macmillan.
Gluckman, M. (1962), 'Les Rites de Passage', in Gluckman M. (ed.), *Essays on the Ritual of Social Relationships*, Manchester: Manchester University Press.
Hart, S. (1991), 'From Property to Person Status: Historical Perspective on Children's Rights', *American Psychologist*, **46**, 1: 53–59.
Hobsbawm, E. (1994), *Age of Extremes: The Short Twentieth Century*, London: Michael Joseph.
Holt, J. (1975), *Escape from Childhood: The Needs and Rights of Children*, Harmondsworth: Penguin.
Hoyles, M. (1979) (ed.), *Changing Childhood*, London: Writers and Readers Co-operative.
James, A. and Prout, A. (1990), *Constructing and Reconstructing Childhood: Contemporary Issues in the Sociological Study of Childhood*, Basingstoke: Falmer Press.
Jones, J.M. and McNeely, R. L. (1981), 'Children's Rights in Historical Perspective', in *Social Development Issues*, Spring 1981, 9–26.

Keniston, K. (1971), *Youth and Dissent: The Rise of the New Opposition*, New York: Harvest.
Lindsay, M.J. (1992), *An Introduction to Children's Rights*, NCB/Barnardo's *Highlight*, no. 113.
Macfarlane, A. (1986), *Marriage and Home in England*, Oxford: Basil Blackwell.
Maslow, A. (1970), *Motivation and Personality*, (2nd edn), New York: Harper and Row.
McLaughlin, M. (1976), 'Survivors and Surrogates: Children and Parents from the 9th to the 13th Centuries', in De Mause, L. (ed.), *The History of Childhood*, London: Souvenir Press.
Mead, M. (1977), *Growing up in New Guinea*, Harmondsworth: Penguin.
Miller, D. (1970), 'Parental Responsibility for Adolescent Maturity', in Elliot, K. (ed.), *The Family and its Future*, London: J. and A. Churchill.
Neill, A.S. (1976), *Summerhill: A radical approach to education*, Harmondsworth: Penguin.
Piaget, J. (1928), *Judgement and Reasoning in the Child*, (translator Warden, M.), London: Kegan, Paul, Trench, Truber & Co.
Pollock, L. (1983), *Forgotten Children: Parent-Child Relationships from 1500 to 1900*, Cambridge: Cambridge University Press.
Selbourne, D. (1994), *The Principle of Duty*, London: Sinclair Stevenson.
Shahar, S. (1992), *Childhood in the Middle Ages*, (translator Galai, C.), London: Routledge.
Stephens, W.N. (1963), *The Family in Cross-Cultural Perspective*, New York: Holt, Rinehart and Winston.
Van Gennep, A. (1960), *The Rites of Passage*, (translator Vizedom M. and Caffee G.), London: Routledge and Kegan Paul .
Wilson, S. (1984), 'The Myth of Motherhood as a Myth: The Historical View of European Child Rearing', *Social History*, **9**, 2: 181–198.

2 Gender matters: man the hunter

ANN OAKLEY

When Pearl Jephcott wrote a book called *Some Young People* in 1954, her concern was to identify the reasons why teenagers were failing to join the youth organizations provided for them by their elders and betters (Jephcott, 1954). The picture revealed by Jephcott's survey hovered on the edge of the emergent youth culture which had become common sociological currency by the 1970s (Hall and Jefferson, 1977; Mungham and Pearson, 1976). Young people wanted to do what they wanted to do, not what adults decreed for them. But the girls in Jephcott's study were strikingly different from the boys. In working-class families particularly, young women were kept home from school or work to help with domestic tasks, and expected to get married as soon as possible. These practices and expectations found their way into the behaviour of the young people, despite the gender-neutral tone of equal opportunities for all that marked the first generation of young people to be brought up in Britain's shining new welfare state.

The questions asked in any survey of young people are different in the 1990s. Time has moved on, and we no longer naively believe that political change will automatically be mirrored in changes in personal behaviour. We know that a public rhetoric of equal opportunity is insufficient to iron out profound social inequalities. But (or therefore) it would appear that the signal power of gender as a social differentiator remains. Many of the answers given by the young people to the *Young People's Social Attitudes Survey* show gender differences, and some of these are commented on in other chapters. The purpose of this chapter is to focus particularly on those sections of the questionnaire that probe attitudes towards the social division of labour by gender, both in the home and out of it, or that otherwise throw some light on gender as an important dimension of young people's experiences.

Away from the traditional family?

Since the 1950s, there have been great changes in many aspects of young people's family lives. Far more of them now grow up in families that do not reflect the 'cereal packet norm' of two married parents living with their biological children (Family Policy Studies Centre, 1994). It is estimated that by the end of the century, half of all British children will not be born to and grow up with their married, biological parents (Kiernan and Wicks, 1990).

British young people share these aspects of their family lives with other European youth, although the speed and the extent of change vary in different countries: in Sweden and Denmark, for example, non-marital cohabitation rates are particularly high; in the Netherlands, the number of single-parent families has actually declined since the 1960s (Hess, 1995: 133, 139).

A total of 30% of the 580 young people who completed the *Young People's Social Attitudes* (YPSA) questionnaire were living in non-nuclear family households at the time they filled in the questionnaires. Twenty-one per cent were living in single-parent families, and 9% were living without their parents in student households, independently or with a partner. Of those living in single-parent households, most (84%) lived with their mothers. This reflects the national pattern, in which 17% of under-sixteens live in single-parent families and 90% of these are headed by women (Family Policy Studies Centre, 1994).

But do young people's views about the morality of different social forms match this changing panorama of family life? According to table 1, there is widespread support for cohabitation both as a substitute and as a preparation for marriage. Most young people think that living together is OK, and that people ought to do this before deciding to get married. Few agree that a bad marriage is better than none at all. About half consider that a single-parent family can do as well as a two-parent one, and most disagree with the notion that having children is a reason for parents to stay together.

There are clear gender differences here, with young men revealing themselves as more conventional and pro-marriage than young women. Most striking of all is the difference between the 66% of young women and the 45% of young men who consider that one parent can be as good as two. Are the young women perhaps sensing here their own very possible trajectories in this direction? Some may also be reflecting on their own positive experiences of being raised by single mothers (Csikszentmihalyi and Larson, 1984).

At the core of the 'traditional' nuclear family is the ideology and practice of women's devotion to housework, childrearing and family care, and men's to the breadwinning role. Table 2 gives the young people's answers to a series of prescriptive statements about gender and family life. Again, the gender differences stand out.

Young men are more likely than young women to agree with the view that men should go out to work and women should stay at home, and to

Table 1. **Attitudes to marriage by gender**

	Agree[1]		**Neither agree nor disagree**		**Disagree**[2]		
	Females	**Males**	**Females**	**Males**	**Females**	**Males**	p^3
	%	%	%	%	%	%	
It is all right for a couple to live together without intending to get married	82	78	10	12	9	9	$p<0.10$
It is good idea for a couple who intend to get married to live together first	79	85	12	10	7	3	$p<0.05$
It is better to have a bad marriage than no marriage at all	3	11	7	8	88	80	$p<0.01$
When there are children in the family, parents should stay together even if they don't get along	14	22	16	25	68	51	$p<0.01$
One parent can bring up a child as well as two parents	66	45	16	16	17	37	$p<0.0001$

[1] This includes young people who 'agreed strongly' with the statement.
[2] This includes young people who 'disagreed strongly' with the statement.
[3] Significance levels (p) on this and following tables were calculated using the chi-square test on a stand-alone statistics pack; levels of $p<0.1$ or less are shown.

Table 2. **The gendering of family life by gender**

	Agree[1]		Neither agree nor disagree		Disagree[2]		
	Females	**Males**	**Females**	**Males**	**Females**	**Males**	***p***
	%	%	%	%	%	%	
A man's job is to earn money; a woman's job is to look after the home and family	7	14	6	16	87	69	$p<0.0001$
It is not good if the man stays at home and cares for the children and the woman goes out to work	10	18	16	25	74	57	$p<0.0001$
A working mother can establish just as warm and secure a relationship with her child as a mother who does not work	75	63	10	15	14	20	$p<0.01$
All in all, family life suffers when the woman has a full time job	27	32	21	24	51	42	$p<0.05$
Family life often suffers because men concentrate too much on their work	42	47	29	26	26	26	NS
Having job is best way for a woman to be an independent person	62	61	23	25	13	11	NS

[1] This includes young people who 'agreed strongly' with the statement.
[2] This includes young people who 'disagreed strongly' with the statement.
NS, not significant.

disagree with the practice of reversing these traditional gender roles. They are significantly less likely to believe that employed mothers are just as capable as non-employed mothers of developing warm and secure relationships with their children, and more likely to take the view that family life suffers if women take paid work outside the home. Somewhat surprisingly, perhaps, the idea that men's focus on their paid work poses a strain for family life draws the support of nearly half of both sexes. There is not much difference, either, in the level of agreement about having a job being the best way for women to be independent — in theory.

Other studies confirm these general findings. Analysing four combined surveys of young people aged 12–22 studied in 1985, Furnham and Gunter reported that young men agreed more readily with the statement that, 'it is wrong for mothers of small children to go out to work', and were more inclined to agree that 'women should worry less about being equal with men and more about becoming good wives and mothers' (Furnham and Gunter, 1989: 95). Questions about the importance of paid work to women reiterated the willingness of both sexes to agree with this in principle, if not in practice. The males in the Furnham and Gunter sample were more sceptical than the females of the need for husbands to share the housework when women go out to work. Twice as many young men as young women considered that a woman's place is still in the home (Furnham and Gunter, 1989: 92, 96).

The limitations of the questions asked mean that it is impossible to guess at the reasons why the young men should be more wedded to traditional notions of the family than young women. There is little evidence that boys react more adversely than girls to family breakup (Fombonne, 1995: 584); on the other hand, we know that men may express negative emotions connected with their personal lives less readily than women. In the study *Young People, Health and Family Life* by Brannen and colleagues, men's concern to maintain the 'public front' of the family as a happy and successfully functioning unit was as impressive as women's interest in freely discussing the details of problems and difficulties in managing families with adolescent children (Brannen *et al.*, 1994).

The *1987 British Social Attitudes* (BSA) *Survey* data on adults' attitudes to gender roles and the family suggest that one place young people may be getting their attitudes from is their parents. Overall, 48% of the adults thought men should go out to work and women should stay at home, 32% that women should not combine paid work and motherhood, and 60% that having a job is the best way for women to be independent (Jowell *et al.*, 1988: 189). A 'traditionalism' scale created out of answers to these questions showed that 36% of men compared with 26% of women held traditional or highly traditional views of gender roles in the family (Jowell *et al.*, 1988:

200). Men were prone to a view that many would consider outdated in the days of 'working mothers' — that mothers of young children should stay at home to look after them.

The data from the 1994 BSA survey indicate changing attitudes towards men's and women's roles. Only 24% of adults thought that a man's job was to earn money and a woman's to look after the home and the family. However, attitudes on whether family life would suffer if women have a full-time job and whether having a job is the best way for women to be independent, remained unaltered since 1987. Thirty-two per cent and 59% of adults, respectively, agreed with these two statements.

Who should do the housework?

As regards who should do different household tasks, the young men in the YPSA survey were consistent in keeping to a traditionalist line: it was evidently more difficult for them to believe that the sexes should share the housework. The questionnaire asked the young people to imagine a man and a woman who are living together, and then went on to pose a series of questions about how family jobs should be shared out in this situation. Table 3 gives their answers. More than 80% of the young women think that making meals, organizing money, shopping, washing, ironing and looking after sick family members should be shared tasks, but the percentages of young men taking this view are significantly lower in every case. The most gendered task is household repairs; only about half the young women and a third of the young men consider this a task to be shared equally. If we look at the third column below, the contours of men's role in the household would appear to be restricted to household repairs and organizing money. Very few young people see housework as something that should be done mainly by men. On the other hand, a core of them do still believe it is women's work (column 2), with the highest percentage here being the 30% of young men who deem women responsible for looking after the sick, and almost as many (26%) who see washing and ironing as uniquely feminine work.

Once again, traces of these views emerge in other studies. Table 4 compares the percentages of the young people surveyed in 1985 in Furnham and Gunter's study with those in the YPSA survey on the level of agreement with the idea of shared household work; the table includes the five tasks covered in both studies: shopping, paying bills, making meals, washing and ironing and household repairs. The rank order of 'shareworthiness' for the young men is the same in both studies, whereas for the young women, making meals jumped from third to first place between the two

Table 3. **The gendering of housework by gender**

	Should be shared equally		**Should be mainly done by: women**		**men**		
	Females %	**Males** %	**Females** %	**Males** %	**Females** %	**Males** %	***p***
Making evening meal	88	74	9	24	2	1	$p<0.0001$
Organizing money and paying bills	85	74	8	10	8	16	$p<0.01$
Grocery shopping	84	75	16	22	<1	3	$p<0.01$
Washing and ironing	82	73	15	26	2	<1	$p<0.01$
Looking after sick family members	83	69	16	30	1	1	$p<0.001$
Household repairs	55	35	2	3	43	62	$p<0.0001$

dates. Another conclusion to be drawn from this table is that in every case the percentage of young people saying a task should be shared increased over the nine-year period between the two studies. By 1994, the 'principled egalitarians' among young men exceeded those among young women in 1985.

Table 4. **Rank ordering of household tasks as 'shareworthy': 1985[1] and 1994[2] data compared** [Rank ordering of 'shareworthiness' (% saying task should be shared)]

	1985 data		**1994 data**	
	Females	**Males**	**Females**	**Males**
Shopping	1 (74)	1 (60)	3 (84)	1 (75)
Paying bills	2 (58)	2 (57)	2 (85)	2 (74)
Making meals	3 (50)	3 (41)	1 (88)	3 (74)
Washing and ironing	4 (38)	4 (33)	4 (82)	4 (73)
Household repairs	5 (34)	5 (32)	5 (55)	5 (35)

[1] Based on *n*=2000 young people aged 12–22 (Furnham and Gunter, 1985).
[2] Based on *n*=580, YPSA survey, 1994.

Household tasks are differently gendered; that is, some are more feminine and some more masculine. Looking after the sick and washing and ironing are aspects of women's health care role in the home that men seem especially reluctant to claim as their own. These are the tasks least likely to be described by either sex in table 3 as suitable for men. The mending and money-organizing roles, on the other hand, fit the masculine gender stereotype — man the builder and financier — much more closely, though money management has been shown to be an aspect of the division of labour marked by different 'systems', particularly in different social classes (Pahl, 1980). One formation, that of women holding the purse strings and giving men back a portion of their wages (or these days, Unemployment Benefit) as pocket money, was celebrated in the Bethnal Green community studies of the 1960s (Young and Willmott, 1957).

The trouble is that prescriptive views — who ought to do what — may not be much reflection of what actually goes on in households. In the 1987 wave of BSA data collection, the percentages of adults saying that people *should* share the six tasks shown in table 3 ranged from 23% for household repairs to 65% for shopping, but the percentages *admitting* to task sharing in practice were in every case substantially lower, ranging from 8% for repairs to 43% for shopping. Interestingly, the rank order in each case was the same; that is, both the prescriptive and the actual descriptions reflected the same hierarchical ordering of gendering, with washing and ironing and household repairs being seen as least shareworthy (Jowell *et al.*, 1988: 184).

The data from the 1994 adult BSA survey show no marked divergence from this hierarchical ordering of task sharing. The range varies from 18% for household repairs and washing and ironing to 52% for shopping, with second place going to 'looking after sick family members' (45%) and third place to 'deciding what to have for dinner' (35%).

Comparing the young people's data with the adult data (1987 and 1994) produces some interesting conclusions. Firstly, and as table 5 shows, the perception of tasks as more or less shareworthy follows broadly similar patterns in the two genders and generations. But, secondly, the generational comparison shows a clear difference: young people, irrespective of gender, espouse a higher degree of prescriptive democracy about housework than adults. For all the tasks, a considerably higher proportion of young people than adults adhere to the idea of sharing as something that *should* happen.

The largest generational increases in prescriptive democracy are for making meals, washing and ironing and household repairs.

Table 5. **Rank ordering of household tasks as 'shareworthy': Young men and women[1] and adult men and women[2]** [Rank ordering of 'shareworthiness' (% saying task should be shared)]

	Young men		Adult men		Young women		Adult women	
Making evening meal	2	(74)	4	(40)	1	(88)	4	(43)
Organizing money and paying bills	3	(74)	2	(58)	2	(85)	2	(65)
Grocery shopping	1	(75)	1	(65)	3	(84)	1	(65)
Washing and ironing	4	(73)	5	(27)	5	(82)	5	(27)
Looking after sick family members	5	(69)	3	(55)	4	(83)	3	(47)
Household repairs	6	(35)	6	(18)	6	(55)	6	(27)

[1] Based on *n*=580, YPSA survey, 1994.
[2] Based on *n*=1437, Witherspoon (1988: 198–99).

Practice versus precept

Unlike those of adults, young people's views about what ought to happen cannot easily be measured against actual practice. The constraints and the context for the housework young people do is, for most of them, the parental home. In the *Young People, Health and Family Life* study, Brannen and colleagues reported housework as a contentious area within households containing teenagers. At 16, young people seemed to be making a diminishing rather than increasing contribution to household work. Mothers were significantly more likely than fathers to say that they themselves did most of the housework, but parents agreed that teenagers did rather little. Mothers were especially vociferous about their dissatisfaction with young people's input. Some of the young people in this study were leaving education and getting jobs, and some of the mothers commented that working teenagers expected to be 'waited on hand and foot', despite the fact that their mothers were often in the labour force as well (Brannen *et al.*, 1994: 53–55). This is not the 'spoiling and keeping close' that Diana Leonard found in her 1980 study, where mothers serviced young people in order to keep them attached to the family later on, when the mothers would be old and might need help (Leonard, 1980). Rather, it is the impotent frustration of women with too much to do meeting head on the recalcitrant and seemingly irrational non-co-operation of the young, who do not regard housework as their proper province. That the chief reason for this behaviour is attitude rather than time is confirmed by studies of young people who leave school and move into unemployment while still living at home. Not having much to do during the day does not mean a greater contribution to the housework (Hutson and Jenkins, 1989). There are parallels here with the 'male defensiveness' that underlies the reluctance of unemployed men to use their spare time productively in household work (Morris, 1990).

International work on children and young people's domestic labour demonstrates a hierarchy of gender and generational inputs to household work: mothers first, followed by girls, followed by boys, followed by fathers (Frones *et al.*, 1992: 37). In the *Young People, Health and Family Life* study, there were statistically significant differences between young men and young women's inputs to 11 out of 13 household tasks (Brannen, 1995: 321). Young women did more in each case, except for gardening and cleaning the windows or the car. The reasons for these differences may be complex. The household interviews carried out in this study pointed to the importance of unequal parental expectations: young women were more than twice as likely as young men to say their parents expected them to help a lot with the housework. Other studies of how young people spend their leisure time show the concentration of young women's leisure time in home-centred activities where 'leisure' is combined with various forms of domestic work. When young men spend leisure time at home, this is more likely to be 'pure leisure' (Deem, 1986). These and other gendered differences in leisure activities are virtually identical whether young people are in education, at work, or unemployed (Wallace and Cross, 1990).

A distinction needs to be made between 'self-care' and 'family-care' tasks. Young people may be expected to clear up their own mess and look after themselves, but not contribute much to general household work. Young women do more 'family-care' than young men (Goodnow, 1988, 1990). For example, in the *Young People, Health and Family Life* study, similar percentages of young women and young men (60% and 57%) made their own meals at least once a week, but 33% of young women and 21% of young men made meals for others (Brannen, 1995).

Qualitative studies put the flesh on the bare bones of these quantitative responses by suggesting some of the ways in which belonging to particular kinds of families may encourage young women to develop patterns of 'family care' and young men to resist these. For example, Bates' ethnographic study of 16–18-year-old girls on a Youth Training Scheme for jobs in institutional care indicates how the girls' adjustment to caring roles at work reinforces the roles they have been taught to occupy at home — roles which are distinctively different from those assigned to their brothers (Bates, 1993).

The YPSA survey did not ask the young people about their actual contribution to the housework — either self-care or family-care. But two questions did ask at what age the young people thought children should be expected to help with the daily washing up and regularly make their own bed. Their answers show a clear tendency for young women to see both these activities as appropriate at younger ages than young men; 37% thought children of nine and younger should help with the washing up and 56% that children of this age should make their own beds. The corresponding figures for the young men were 25% and 42% as shown in table 6.

Table 6. **Age at which people should be expected to help with the washing up and regularly make their own bed**

	Females		**Males**	
	Washing up	**Making bed**	**Washing up**	**Making bed**
	%	%	%	%
≤9	37	56	25	42
10–12	46	34	48	39
13–15	10	6	17	11
16 or more	3	<1	4	4

Gender difference for washing up, $p<0.01$, and for making beds, $p<0.001$.

As Tony Newman discusses in Chapter 1, a series of questions about the age at which people should be allowed to engage in a range of various activities yielded gendered responses for babysitting young children, being left alone for an evening, and driving a car on a public road. The young women thought that babysitting, and the young men that being left alone and driving, could be done at younger ages. There were, interestingly, no significant gender differences for voting age, leaving home or school, having sex, buying alcohol, watching cinema films, getting married or getting a part-time job.

The world outside the home

If the world inside the home is subject to prescriptive and actual differences by gender, what about the world outside it? It would not be surprising if the young people's views about the difference gender makes to parental roles were reflected in their norms about the performance of occupational roles outside the home. And so, indeed, we find that occupations differ in the extent to which they are perceived as being suitable for both men and women as described in table 7.

Being a family doctor or a member of parliament lead the list of 'shareworthy' jobs, followed by being a bank manager, nursing and policing, with flying 'planes and being a car mechanic or a secretary coming bottom of the list. As before, there are significant differences in young men's and young women's answers for all the occupations except being an MP and a bank manager. Nursing and policing and being a car mechanic stand out as more shareworthy in female than male eyes. Young men's fondness for cars perhaps fits with their view that driving at young ages is something they should be allowed to do.

Other surveys of young people's perceptions of different occupations again testify to the greater tendency of young men to hold sexist views of the occupational structure. Furnham and Gunter, for example, found that more young women believed in completely equal opportunities in getting jobs and being promoted, whereas young men were more inclined to the belief that men could do many jobs better than women, and were more prone to take a dim view of women's ability to handle positions of responsibility (Furnham and Gunter, 1989: 94).

Table 7. **The gendering of paid work**

	Suitable for:						
	Both men & women		**Women more**		**Men more**		
	Females %	**Males** %	**Females** %	**Males** %	**Females** %	**Males** %	***p***
GP	97	89	1	5	2	6	$p<0.01$
MP	90	90	1	1	7	9	NS
Bank manager	91	89	1	<1	8	11	NS
Nurse	87	74	12	25	0	<1	$p<0.001$
Police officer	89	79	<1	<1	11	20	$p<0.01$
Airline pilot	71	66	<1	3	28	32	$p<0.10$
Car mechanic	69	45	0	<1	31	54	$p<0.0001$
Secretary	60	49	40	50	0	<1	$p<0.05$

NS, not significant.

Once again, data from the BSA adult survey in 1987 provide a basis for comparison for seven of the eight occupations shown in the table above (airline pilot was not on the list for the adult survey in 1987). The adult ranking of shareworthy occupations in 1987 was as follows: GP (93%), MP (89%), bank manager (70%), police officer (62%), secretary (44%), nurse (31%) and car mechanic (31%).

The data from the 1994 BSA survey differ from the 1987 survey in only one respect, which is that 72% of adults regarded the occupation of a nurse to be equally suitable for both men and women, thus placing the occupation of a nurse between that of a bank manager (81%) and police officer (67%) in the ranking of shareworthy occupations. The adults in the 1994 survey were also asked their views on the occupation of an airline pilot and 54% regarded this occupation as suitable for both men and women. The rank order for shareworthiness obtained in 1994 is thus: GP, MP, bank manager, nurse, police officer, airline pilot, secretary and car mechanic.

This compares with the very similar rankings obtained in the YPSA survey for young women shown in table 7 (GP, MP, bank manager, police officer, nurse, car mechanic and secretary) and for young men (MP, GP, bank manager, police officer, nurse, secretary and car mechanic). A comparison of the adult data for 1994, 1987 and 1984 showed increases in the number of 'principled egalitarians' for all these jobs (Jowell *et al.*, 1988: 179–80). It is significant that, as with the case for prescriptive views of household tasks, the 1994 percentages of 'principled egalitarians' among young people shown in table 7 are in every case higher than for adults. This suggests a continuing trend in the direction of perceived equality — the view that being a man or a woman is largely irrelevant to the requirements of particular jobs. But, like the data for housework, this, of course, says nothing about how jobs are divided in practice, nor about how the young people themselves may or may not translate their values about occupational equality into their own future job choices. All the indications are that gender segregation persists as a structural feature of the labour market in Britain and other countries, and is likely to remain so (Scott, 1994).

Ambitions and priorities

The statistics of occupational gender segregation and of parenting and household responsibilities suggest that, whatever young people feel ought to happen, they are likely to find themselves as adults living in a social world marked by significant gender inequalities. Although there has been a substantial narrowing of the gender gap since the 1960s, recent gains have been incremental only. Women continue to specialize in part-time work, and in low-earning service jobs (Equal Opportunities Commission, 1995). Women's place in the world outside the home reflects traditional attitudes to gender and work, and their much greater commitment of time and resources to the home. The gender division of labour is connected in complex and poorly understood ways to men's and women's mental and physical health (Wingard, 1984). It seems that employment and the family operate differently as protective factors for men's and women's health; the family is better for men, and employment is better for women (Gove and Tudor, 1973; Popay *et al.*, 1993; Verbrugge, 1988). Studies of women's experiences (there have been few of men) with their 'two roles' show a good deal of dissatisfaction with the effort and personal disadvantages of combining the two (Dean, 1992). Perhaps men's and women's underlying aims and priorities demonstrate more similarities than their trajectories through life might suggest?

The data in table 8 certainly point to a greater commonality of attitude between young men and women than the other data from the YPSA survey drawn on in this chapter. The young people were asked which of a checklist of ambitions they would pick as their main one in life.

Table 8. **Main ambition in life by gender**

	Females %	**Males** %	***p***
To be happy	47	40	$p<0.0001$
To be well off	3	14	$p<0.0001$
To have good health	8	5	NS
To have a good job	12	12	NS
To be successful at work	11	9	NS
To have my own home	<1	2	NS
To have a family	9	10	NS
To travel and see the world	11	7	$p<0.10$

NS, not significant.

The results show that 'to be happy' comes first with both sexes as a main ambition, and considerably ahead of any others. Significantly, for a generation brought up with the materialistic values of successive Conservative governments, being well off, having a good job and success at work are not high priorities, although the young men put being well off somewhat higher than the young women. The slightly higher figure for young women wanting to travel and see the world may reflect their perception of constrictions awaiting them in their adult lives. Annoyingly for all those well-meaning health educators who labour to persuade young people to cut risk-taking activities such as smoking, drinking and drug-taking, for over 90% of both sexes having good health is not something to be prized as a goal.

These answers echo those of other studies, particularly as regards the low priority young people attach to health, and the high regard in which they hold personal happiness. For example, in the young people, health and family life study, 33% of young women and 30% of young men said happiness was the most important thing in life for them, and 10% and 15% respectively acknowledged that good health was important (SSRU/TCRU, 1995). Findings from these other studies also indicate that young people may be more attached to the value of a happy family life than stereotypical images of conflictual youth might suggest. Almost one in five young women in the young people, health and family life sample said that a happy family was the most important thing in life for them; for a third of a sample of 820 15-year-olds from whom data were collected in 1981, the family was actually more important than their friends, though young women in the latter study showed a stronger attachment than young men to their families as sources of enjoyment (Simmons and Wade, 1984: 125, 168).

As we all know, the answers you get depend on the questions you ask. Table 9 gives the answers of the YPSA survey to the slightly different question of how certain key features of people's personal circumstances are thought to figure in their chances of doing 'well in life'. This question asked the young people to reflect a little more on what actually happens, as distinct from what they might wish to happen. In matching ambition to reality, what do young people perceive to be the constraints and the facilitators? Table 9 shows that the ranking of 'very important' is the same for both sexes: a good education, hard work, and a wealthy family, with race and being born male or female having least influence.

In these respects, at least, these young people carry the values of Thatcher's generation — though some might say that a good education is increasingly hard to find. The greater propensity of young men to value education shown in this table reflects continued differences between men and women in the educational sphere (Equal Opportunities Commission, 1995).

Table 9. **Importance of certain factors in doing well in life**

	Very important[1]		Fairly Important		Not Important[2]		
	Females	Males	Females	Males	Females	Males	*p*
	%	%	%	%	%	%	
Coming from a wealthy family	13	15	23	36	64	50	$p<0.05$
Having a good education	76	83	23	15	1	2	$p<0.05$
Hard work	69	76	28	22	2	1	$p<0.10$
A person's race	11	11	14	17	75	73	$p<0.10$
Being a man or a woman	6	7	13	13	81	81	NS

[1] This includes young people who chose the response 'essential'.
[2] This includes young people who chose the response 'not at all important'.
NS, not significant.

The public and the private

The traditional divide in gender roles is between women's roles in the private sphere and men's in the public. As we have seen, the theme of the public/private divide is still very much present in young people's attitudes. The home and the family continue to have an importance for young women, both in practice and in prospect, which is qualitatively different from the meaning invested in them by young men. The YPSA data also suggest that the world outside the home remains a more foreign and frightening place for young women.

As Diana McNeish discusses in greater detail in Chapter 4, the section of the questionnaire dealing with experience of, and attitudes towards, crime reveals that, although young men are more likely than young women to have been physically attacked and/or threatened, it is women who exhibit the greatest fear of crime, and who most tend to take precautions against becoming victims. A total of 76% of the young women (67% of men) said they are careful to lock up the home when they go out; 16% (7% of young men) do not answer the door. Most strikingly, 30% of young women but only 12% of young men avoid going out on their own because of the risk of crime. Overall, 67% of young women (56% of men) worry about becoming a crime victim.

Although there is no difference in the likelihood of personally knowing a victim of crime, young women are significantly more likely to react to this knowledge by becoming more afraid (35% versus 20% of young men). Interestingly, questions about what could be done to reduce crime reveal few gender differences, except that more young women than men (60% versus 44%) think that having less crime and violence on television would be an effective remedy.

The conceptual division between fear of crime and actual risk is echoed in other studies of adults (Garofalo and Laub, 1981), which also demonstrate women's greater fearfulness and a general trend towards increased fear over time (Hough and Mayhew, 1985; Furnham and Gunter, 1989).

Conclusion

Although the young people in this study disclaimed the importance of being born male or female as a shaper of life experience, much of what they said told a rather different story. On many questions, the young men's answers were significantly different from the young women's. It seems, then, that the social processes embedded in the cultural assignation to masculine or feminine gender still have a great deal of power to influence experiences, values, perceptions and ambitions. The experiences and underlying beliefs and values glimpsed through the ecliptic lens of the YPSA survey questions do not suggest an androgynous youth culture. What they suggest, instead, is a pattern of endemic difference, and a continued fundamental tension between the ideology of gender equality, on the one hand, and the realities of learning to live in a gendered world, on the other.

The classic studies of young people carried out in the 1970s and 80s delineated a basic intermeshing of class and gender stereotyping in youth culture which gave rise to 'typical girls' who were channelled into working-class feminine jobs, and 'real boys' who asserted their masculinity by being rough and eschewing anything feminine, including, particularly housework and anything that smacks of caring (Griffin, 1985; Willis, 1977). One might have expected post-Fordist production patterns, together with new systems of education and training, and the greater political emphasis on individual self-realization, to have changed all this. But, on the contrary, gender remains a significant influence on youth transitions. The themes emerging in this chapter are confirmed by the statistics of young people's post-sixteen careers. Although more young women stay in education, fewer go on to higher education (Redpath and Harvey, 1987). Those who get jobs or take youth training enter a more restricted occupational world. Raffe and Courtney (1988), for example, found that more than half the girls in their survey worked in the two occupational categories of clerical and personal services, and that two more — selling and materials processing — accounted for most of the rest. The other 12 categories were largely a male preserve.

The background to this chapter is rather little critical sociological research on the significance of gender in the transition to adulthood, particularly in the area of gender and household work. With the increase in youth unemployment that has taken place over the last 20 years, and changes in youth policy towards greater intervention in young people's lives, the focus of research and enquiry has been on employment and the labour market rather than on the domestic lives of young people. Within the study of domestic life, investigators have concentrated on the adult division of labour. There has also been a tendency to conceive of the framework for the study of housework as being narrowly the two-parent-and-dependent-child nuclear family. Wider kinship networks, and their role in the construction of household work, have been neglected. Dominant conceptions of childhood have emphasized the relative passivity and incompetence of the child and young person regarding the performance of adult tasks (Alderson, 1990).

The literature tends to be marked by two contrary assumptions: that gender is insignificant; and that the trajectories of young men and young women are bound to be different, and therefore unremarkable, in commonsense ways. Commonly held 'adultist' images of young people portray them as in revolt against parental authority and experiencing crises of conflict as a 'natural' stage in their development (Rutter *et al.*, 1976). These images suggest that countering parental attitudinal and behavioural patterns may be part of the process of growing up (Davis, 1990). But the data drawn on in this chapter suggest a different interpretation. As regards gender differences, young people are, to a large extent, speaking exactly the same language as their parents, albeit in slightly muted tones. This mismatch between what young people actually say and what adults think they believe and do may be only one of many contrasts laid bare by survey data (Coleman, 1990).

Gender is, of course, only one axis of differentiation between the experiences of different groups of young people; class and ethnicity can be equally important (Bates and Riseborough, 1993). Beyond all these social divisions and questions about their meaning, it is important not to lose sight of the main themes that emerge from this survey of young people's lives today. One example is crime. The fact that 82% of these young people have already been the victim of at least one crime, and that 79% feel either very unsafe, a bit unsafe or only fairly safe going out after dark says something highly significant about the kind of society in which they are growing up. Similarly, the fact that 82% report bullying at school, around 90% think that British society is prejudiced against Asians and black people, 60% say they are not interested in politics, and 57% worry about being unable to get a job at the end of their education all pose serious questions about the legacy of post-war culture that this generation of young people has inherited. Whereas in the mid 1970s, most young people went straight from education to work, the youth labour market has now virtually collapsed (Wallace and Cross, 1990). The problem of youth unemployment is in many ways 'the central issue of the youth question' (Davis, 1990: 214). In combination with young people's concerns for environmental issues, the impact of poverty on themselves and their families, and the global threat of nuclear war (Solantaus 1987, 1991), questions about who does what in the home may seem only trivially important. But at another level, global and the domestic issues are interconnected. Systematic variations in life opportunities and ideologies by gender represent one form of social discrimination. A society characterized by gender discrimination is also likely to be one that is unequal in other ways.

References

Alderson, P. (1990), *Choosing for Children*, Oxford: Oxford University Press.

Bates, I. (1993), 'A job which is "right for me"?' in Bates, I. and Riseborough, G. (eds), *Youth and Inequality*, Buckingham: Open University Press.

Bates, I. and Riseborough, G. (1993), (eds), *Youth and Inequality*, Buckingham: Open University Press.

Brannen, J. (1995), 'Young people and their contribution to household work', *Sociology*, **29**, 2: 317–38.

Brannen, J., Dodd, K., Oakley, A. and Storey, P. (1994) *Young People, Health and Family Life,* Buckingham: Open University Press.

Coleman, J. (1990), *The Nature of Adolescence*, (2nd edn), London: Routledge.

Csikszentmihalyi, M. and Larson, R. (1984), *Being Adolescent: Conflict and growth in the teenage years*, New York: Basic Books.

Davis, J. (1990), *Youth and the Condition of Britain*, London: The Athlone Press.

Dean, K. (1992), 'Double burdens of work: The female work and health paradox', *Health Promotion International*, **7**, 1: 17–25.

Deem, R. (1986), *All Work and No Play?*, Milton Keynes: Open University Press.

Equal Opportunities Commission (1995), *Some Facts About Women*, Manchester: EOC.

Family Policy Studies Centre (1994), *Factsheet 1: Putting families on the map*, London: Family Policy Studies Centre.

Fombonne, E. (1995), 'Depressive disorders: Time trends and possible explanatory mechanisms', in Rutter, M. and Smith, D.J., (eds), *Psychosocial Disorders in Young People*, Chichester: John Wiley.

Frones, I., Jensen, A. and Solberg, A. (1992), *National Report for Norway. Childhood as a Social Phenomenon Project*, Eurosocial Report 36/1, European Centre, Bergasse 17, 1090 Vienna, Austria.

Furnham, A. and Gunter, B. (1989), *The Anatomy of Adolescence: Young People's Social Attitudes in Britain*, London: Routledge.

Garofalo, J. and Laub, J. (1981), 'The fear of crime: broadcasting over perspective', *Victimology: An international journal*, **3**: 242–53.
Goodnow, J. (1988) 'Children's work: Its nature and functions', *Psychological Bulletin*, **103**: 5–26.
Goodnow, J. (1990), 'Children's household work as a base for comparing generations, families and cultures', in Keats, D.M. and Mann, L. (eds), *Heterogeneity in Cross-Cultural Psychology*, Amsterdam: Swets and Zeitlinger.
Gove, W.S. and Tudor, J.F. (1973), 'Adult sex roles and mental illness', *American Journal of Sociology*, **78**: 50–73.
Griffin, C. (1985), *Typical Girls*, London: Routledge.
Hall, S. and Jefferson, T. (1977), *Resistance Through Rituals*. London: Hutchinson.
Hess, L.E. (1995) 'Changing family patterns in Western Europe: Opportunity and risk factors for adolescent development', in Rutter, M. and Smith, D.J. (eds), *Psychosocial Disorders in Young People*, Chichester: John Wiley.
Hough, M. and Mayhew, P. (1985), *Taking Account of Crime: Key findings from the 1984 British Crime Survey*, London: HMSO.
Hutson, S. and Jenkins, R. (1989), *Taking the Strain: Families, unemployment and the transition to adulthood*, Milton Keynes: Open University Press.
Jephcott, P. (1954), *Some Young People*: A study of adolescent boys and girls, London: Allen and Unwin.
Jowell, R., Witherspoon, S. and Brook, L. (1988), (eds), *British Social Attitudes: the 5th report*, London: Gower.
Kiernan, K. and Wicks, M. (1990), *Family Change and Future Policy*, London: Family Policy Studies Centre.
Leonard, D. (1980), *Sex and Generation*, London: Tavistock.
Morris, L. (1990), *The Workings of the Household*, Cambridge: Polity Press.
Mungham, G. and Pearson, G. (eds) (1976), *Working Class Youth Culture*, London: Routledge.
Pahl, J. (1980), 'Patterns of money management within marriage', *Journal of Social Policy*, **9**, 3: 313–35.
Popay, J., Bartley, M. and Owen, C. (1993), 'Gender inequalities in health: social position, affective disorders and minor physical morbidity', *Social Science and Medicine*, **36**, 1: 21–32.
Raffe, D. and Courtney, G. (1988), '16–18 on both sides of the border', in Raffe, D. (ed.), *Education and the Youth Labour Market*, Lewes: Falmer Press.
Redpath, B. and Harvey, B. (1987), *Young People's Intentions to enter Higher Education*, London: HMSO.
Rutter, M., Graham, P., Chadwick, O. and Yule, W. (1976), 'Adolescent turmoil: Fact or fiction?', *Journal of Child Psychology and Psychiatry*, **17**: 35–56.
Scott, A.M. (1994), (ed), *Gender Segregation and Social Change*, Oxford: Oxford University Press.
Simmons, C. and Wade, W. (1984), *I Like to Say What I Think*, London: Kogan Page.
SSRU/TCRU (1995), Unpublished data from the young people, health and family life study. London, Social Science Research Unit and Thomas Coram Research Unit.
Solantaus, T. (1987), 'Hopes and worries of young people in three European countries', *Health Promotion*. **2**, 1: 19–27.
Solantaus, T. (1991), 'Young people and the threat of nuclear war: "Out there is a world I belong to". A literature review', *Medicine and War*. **7** (suppl 1): 1–95.
Verbrugge, L. (1988), 'Unveiling higher morbidity for men: the story', in Riley, M.W. (ed.), *Social Structures and Human Lives*, Newbury Park: Sage Publications.
Wallace, C. and Cross, M. (1990), (eds), *Youth in Transition: The sociology of youth and youth policy*, Basingstoke: Falmer Press.

Willis, P. (1977), *Learning to Labour*, Farnborough: Saxon House.
Wingard, D.L. (1984), 'The sex differentials in morbidity, mortality and life style', in Breslow, L., Fielding, J.E. and Lave, L.B. (eds), *Annual Review of Public Health*, **5**:433–458. Palo Alto, California: Annual Reviews Inc.
Witherspoon, S. (1988), 'Interim report: A Woman's Work' in Jowell, R., Witherspoon, S. and Brook, L., (eds), *British Social Attitudes, the 5th Report*, Aldershot: Gower.
Young, M. and Willmott, P. (1957), *Family and Kinship in East London*, London: Routledge.

3 Racial prejudice and racial discrimination: whither British youth?

DARSHAN SACHDEV

The subject of 'race' in multi-racial Britain attracts highly charged views and attitudes which are often negative. These strong attitudes which can precipitate racial prejudice can have a strong behavioural outcome in racial discrimination. The recipients of racial prejudice and racial discrimination are, in the main, those racial groups settled in Britain who are distinguished from the white community by the colour of their skin and by the culture which dictates their mode of dress, dietary practices and customs — 'colour racism' and 'cultural racism' are the terms Modood (1994) has used to distinguish racism resulting from the former from that arising from the latter. Asians (Indians, Pakistanis and Bangladeshis) and black people from Africa and the Caribbean have been the target of prejudice and discrimination in particular since the early 1950s when immigration from the Caribbean and South Asia was encouraged by the British government, which needed to recruit a cheap labour force for its industries at a time of great economic expansion and acute labour shortage.

Britain's multi-racial society has come a long way since the 'first wave' of immigrants from Asia and the Caribbean settled in Britain and encountered racial prejudice and discrimination. The Race Relations Act was introduced in 1965 in response to increasing pressure to tackle racial discrimination. It was strengthened in 1968 and replaced by the 1976 Act (Gordon and Newnham, 1986; Solomos, 1989). This reshaping of the anti-discrimination legislation was intended to control discrimination on the basis of the colour of someone's skin by making it unlawful. In addition, it imposed a statutory duty on local authorities to eliminate racial discrimination. This, in turn, was instrumental in the development and implementation of equal opportunities policies at local levels to provide a framework within which the discriminatory practices against minority ethnic communities could be identified and eradicated.

Notwithstanding these measures taken both at national and at local level, racial prejudice and racial discrimination remain an integral part of the lives of many Asian and African Caribbean people living in Britain today. They have engendered considerable interest and have been commented on by Bagley and Verma (1979), Reeves (1982), Davey (1983), Pilkington (1984), and Armstrong (1989) among others. The consequences of racial prejudice and discrimination in the lives of Asians and African-Caribbean people have been extensively studied, especially in the spheres of housing, education, employment, immigration, health and social services. The surveys conducted by the Policy Studies Institute and the Labour Force Surveys with samples from minority ethnic communities have provided opportunities for analyses of the effects of racial prejudice and racial discrimination on Asian and black communities settled in Britain (Daniel, 1968; Smith, 1976; Brown, 1984; Jones, 1993).

Despite the impressive body of literature in this area, there is a dearth of information about the views and attitudes held by young people in Britain on the issues of racial prejudice and racial discrimination. The *Young People's Social Attitudes* (YPSA) *Survey* begins to bridge this information gap.

This chapter considers, on the basis of survey findings, the extent and direction of the views and attitudes of young people in the areas of racial prejudice, inter-racial marriages, perceived discrimination in the job market against Asians and black people, perceived discrimination in the judicial system, anti-discriminatory legislation, racial prejudice in five years' time and the importance of race in getting ahead in life. This chapter also looks at how well the attitudes of young people coincide with the adults in the same household, usually a parent, interviewed for the *British Social Attitudes* (BSA) *Survey.*

The discussion of survey data below includes the differences between boys and girls in different age groups; the influence of political party identity on attitudes towards racial prejudice and discrimination; and, where possible, comparison of the views and attitudes of young people with those of adult respondents interviewed for the BSA survey in 1994 and in previous years.

The ethnic composition of the respondents

The sample of respondents interviewed for the YPSA survey comprised 92% (532) young people who described themselves as white, 6% (32) young people who described themselves as Asian (Indian, Pakistani or Asian other) and 1% (6) young people who described themselves as black (African or Caribbean origin). Since the number of respondents of Asian or African-Caribbean origin interviewed for the survey was very small, no inferences can be drawn from the data collected from these young people on the views and attitudes of young Asian and black people in general. These data can, however, give a basis for informed speculation.

Views on racial prejudice

One of the earliest definitions of 'prejudice' was penned by Hazlitt, in the early nineteenth century, who suggested that prejudice, "is prejudging any question without having sufficiently examined it, and adhering to our opinion upon it through ignorance, malice or perversity, in spite of every evidence to the contrary" (quoted in Bethlehem, 1985: 2). More than a century later, Reeves (1982), in his evaluative review of 'prejudice' asserted that the term prejudice, "is most commonly used in the field of race or ethnic relations, in the negative sense of 'prejudice against', and applies to unreasonable, unwarranted and hostile attitudes towards racial or ethnic groups."

The prevalence of racial prejudice and its behavioural concomitant, racial discrimination, among British adults was explored in detail in the first BSA survey in 1983. Many of the questions have been asked in subsequent BSA surveys, thus providing useful trend data. A number of these questions were included in the 1994 YPSA survey, affording us the opportunity to compare adults' views on racial prejudice and discrimination over the last few years with the views of young people in 1994.

The YPSA survey has attempted to elicit the extent to which the young people perceive racial prejudice in the wider British society and see themselves as being prejudiced against Asians and black people.

Perceived prejudice against Asian and black people

Airey (1984), in the first BSA report, noted that, "90% of the population believe there is prejudice against Asians and blacks" and that, "younger people (those aged 18–34), who are less likely than older people to express prejudice themselves, are particularly pessimistic about the growth of race prejudice in Britain". He also found that over a third of the adult sample admitted to being prejudiced themselves.

The first of the findings reported by Airey was in response to two parallel questions about Asians and black people, which were also asked in the YPSA survey.

> *Thinking of* **Asians** *(that is people whose families were originally from India, Pakistan and Bangladesh) and* **black** *people (that is people whose families were originally from the West Indies or Africa) who now live in Britain. Do you think there is a lot of prejudice against them in Britain nowadays, a little or hardly any?*

The table below compares the responses of adult respondents in the BSA surveys in 1987, 1991 and 1994 with those given by young respondents in the YPSA survey.

Perceived prejudice against:

	Asian people				**black people**			
	Adults			**Young people**	**Adults**			**Young people**
	1987	**1991**	**1994**	**1994**	**1987**	**1991**	**1994**	**1994**
	%	%	%	%	%	%	%	%
A lot	62	58	59	51	57	50	47	39
A little	30	35	34	41	33	41	44	49
Hardly any	6	4	5	6	7	7	8	10

Source: 1987, 1991 and 1994: BSA surveys.

Around half of the young respondents think that there is 'a lot' of prejudice against Asian people compared with almost six out of every 10 adults interviewed in 1994. In comparison, about four out of 10 young people compared with around five out of 10 adults think that there is 'a lot' of prejudice against black people. However, almost half of the young respondents thought that there was 'a little' prejudice against black people compared with about four in 10 who thought that there was 'a little' prejudice against Asians.

Almost nine out of 10 young people interviewed thought that there was either 'a lot' or 'a little' prejudice against both Asians and black people. The same holds true for adults interviewed in 1987, 1991 and 1994. This suggests that although there are slight differences in the degree and extent of perceived prejudice against Asians and black people by both adults and young people, the total extent of perceived prejudice against these two minority ethnic groups has remained almost constant over time *and* across the two generations interviewed in 1994. The difference between adults and young people in the perceived prejudice against the two minority ethnic groups is thus eroded when the total extent of prejudice ('a lot' and 'a little') is compared.

This comparison of adult responses over the last seven years and young people's responses in 1994 also shows that the differential between the greatest degree of perceived prejudice ('a lot') towards Asians and black people has increased from five percentage points in 1987 (adult data) to 12 percentage points in 1994 (for both adults and young people).

The data from the YPSA survey were examined for gender differences in perceived prejudice against Asians and black people and the results are shown in the next table.

Gender differences in perceived prejudice against:

	Asian people		**black people**	
	Male	**Female**	**Male**	**Female**
	%	%	%	%
A lot	45	57	36	44
A little	46	36	50	46
Hardly any	7	6	13	8

Many more girls than boys thought that there was 'a lot' of prejudice against Asians and black people. Moreover, a greater number of girls perceived 'a lot' of prejudice against Asians than against black people. The perceived prejudice against Asian and black people was found to vary according to the age of the young respondent as the following table shows.

Age differences in perceived prejudice against:

	Asian people			**black people**		
	12–15	**16–17**	**18–19**	**12–15**	**16–17**	**18–19**
	%	%	%	%	%	%
A lot	46	54	66	38	39	43
A little	45	42	26	49	51	45
Hardly any	7	4	7	10	9	12

Of those aged 18 to 19 years, 66% thought that there was 'a lot' of prejudice against Asian people compared with 46 per cent of the 12–15-year-old respondents. The same pattern emerges for respondents across the three age groups who thought there was 'a lot' of prejudice against black people, although the figures are much lower than for Asian people. The differential between the greatest degree of perceived prejudice ('a lot') towards Asians and black people is greatest (23 percentage points) for the 18–19 age group and the smallest for the youngest age group (8 percentage points).

To ascertain whether identification with or support of any one political party was associated with the levels of perceived prejudice against Asians and black people, the young people's responses were grouped by political party identity.

Party political differences in perceived prejudice against:

	Asian people			black people		
	Conserva-tives	Labour	Liberal Democrats	Conserva-tives	Labour	Liberal Democrats
	%	%	%	%	%	%
A lot	51	57	39	30	46	32
A little	46	36	57	60	44	54
Hardly any	1	5	4	8	9	14

Labour identifiers appear to show a greater awareness of the existence of 'a lot' of prejudice against both Asian and black people. About one-half of Conservative supporters and four in 10 of Liberal Democrat supporters thought that there was 'a lot' of prejudice against Asians. Irrespective of the political party young people support, they perceive more prejudice against Asians than against black people. Conservative identifiers, moreover, appear particularly strong in their perception that a much greater degree of prejudice is suffered by Asians than black people.

Self-rated levels of prejudice

The young people were then asked to rate their own levels of racial prejudice. Their responses are compared, in the next table, with those of the adults asked the following question in 1994, and in the previous BSA surveys in 1987 and 1991.

> *How would you describe yourself — as very prejudiced against people of other races, a little prejudiced, or not prejudiced at all?*

Around a quarter of young people claimed they were only 'a little' prejudiced compared with around a third of the adults interviewed in 1994, which is a slight increase in reported prejudice levels by adults since 1991. This difference between the responses of the adult respondents and the young people raises the question of whether the young people are *in fact* less prejudiced than adults or whether they wish to appear less prejudiced. Only systematic research on this issue can answer this question with any degree of confidence.

Self-rated prejudice against people of other races:

	by adults			by young people
	1987	**1991**	**1994**	**1994**
	%	%	%	%
Very prejudiced	4	2	2	2
A little prejudiced	34	29	34	26
Not prejudiced at all	60	68	63	70

Source: 1987, 1991 and 1994: BSA surveys.

Age and gender differences in the responses of young people were examined next.

Age and gender differences in self-rated prejudice against people of other races:

	by males			by females		
	12–15	**16–17**	**18–19**	**12–15**	**16–17**	**18–19**
	%	%	%	%	%	%
Very prejudiced	3	6	0	2	0	2
A little prejudiced	26	43	30	17	23	34
Not prejudiced at all	70	51	70	80	77	64

A greater proportion of 16–17-year-old boys and 18–19-year-old girls admitted to being either 'a lot' or 'a little' prejudiced compared with boys and girls in the other age groups. Fewer girls aged 12–15 years admitted to being 'a little' prejudiced compared with boys of same age. Only about one-half of 16–17-year-old boys stated that they were not prejudiced as opposed to around three-quarters of the girls of same age. Fewer girls of 18–19 described themselves as 'not prejudiced at all' than girls aged 12–17 years.

Attitudes of white people to inter-racial marriages

The issue of racial prejudice against Asians and black people becomes more sharply focused when people's attitudes towards inter-racial marriages are explored. Young (1992) claimed that "we may come closer to eliciting 'actual' prejudice when we ask rather sharper questions about how people would react to the admission of people from ethnic minority groups ... into the intimacy of the family".

Attitudes towards inter-racial marriages are changing and people are apparently more willing than they were in 1989 to accept their close relatives marrying a person of another race, according to a recent survey commissioned by the *Daily Express* (August 9, 1995). When asked "Are there any racial groups that you would not want your son or daughter to marry?", 20% of white respondents said they would not want marriages between their son/daughter and Afro-Caribbeans, 24% objected to marriages with Indians, whereas 28% did not want their son or daughter to marry a Pakistani. Overall, however, about six in 10 British people said they would marry someone from another race — or would not object to their son or daughter doing so.

In the YPSA survey, young respondents were asked two separate questions about marriage and Asian and black people:

> *Do you think* **most** *white people would mind or not mind if one of their close relatives were to marry a person of Asian/black or West Indian origin?*
> *And you personally? Would you mind or not mind?*

The table below compares the responses from white young people with those from white adults in 1994 and in earlier BSA surveys conducted in 1986, 1989 and 1991.

% saying <u>most</u> white people would mind 'a lot' or 'a little':

	Adult respondents				Young respondents
	1986	**1989**	**1991**	**1994**	**1994**
Asian person in family	79	80	74	72	54
Black person in family	76	78	75	73	59

Source: 1986, 1989, 1991 and 1994: BSA surveys.

A much lower percentage of young people compared with adults think that most white people would mind ('a lot' or 'a little') either an Asian or a black person marrying into their family.

When respondents were asked if they themselves would mind (results shown in table below), adults and young people alike claimed to be more accepting than 'most' people. This is in accordance with the earlier findings in respect of perceived prejudice that people perceive others to be more prejudiced than themselves.

% of white respondents saying they would mind 'a lot' or 'a little':

	Adult respondents				**Young respondents**
	1986	**1989**	**1991**	**1994**	**1994**
Asian person in family	50	49	43	37	17
Black person in family	46	52	44	37	15

Source: 1986, 1989, 1991 and 1994: BSA surveys.

The data for adults show, once again, a downward trend, with the young people apparently less prejudiced towards inter-racial marriages than adults. Around two in 10 young people said they would either mind 'a lot' or 'a little' compared with about four in 10 adults, interviewed in 1994.

The age and gender differences in attitudes of white young people to inter-racial marriage were also explored.

% of white young respondents who would mind a relative marrying an Asian:

	Male respondents			**Female respondents**		
	12–15	**16–17**	**18–19**	**12–15**	**16–17**	**18–19**
A lot	7	14	0	6	3	2
A little	10	12	18	10	12	11
Not mind	81	70	82	83	85	82

Although 14% of 16–17-year-old boys said they would mind 'a lot' if a relative married an Asian, none of the oldest boys said they would mind 'a lot'. The oldest girls appear to be most accepting of inter-racial marriages in their family, as only 13% said they would mind either 'a lot' or 'a little'. The 16–17 year age band presents a surprising contrast between boys and girls: 85% of girls in this age group stated that they would not mind compared with 70% of boys.

The data in respect of a relative marrying a black person reveal essentially the same pattern.

% of white young respondents who would mind a relative marrying a black person:

	Male respondents			**Female respondents**		
	12–15	**16–17**	**18–19**	**12–15**	**16–17**	**18–19**
A lot	7	8	0	4	3	4
A little	11	16	12	6	10	14
Not mind	78	73	88	86	87	82

While 16–17-year-old boys appear to be least accepting of a relative marrying a black person, the oldest boys appear to be most accepting (out of the six groups shown in the table). Around a quarter of 16–17-year-old boys said they would mind 'a lot' or 'a little' compared with 12% of the oldest boys. The latter group also had the highest percentage of young people who said they would 'not mind' at all if a relative married a black person. On the other hand, of the three age groups for girls, the youngest girls claimed to be most accepting of a relative marrying a black person and the oldest girls appear to be least accepting — 10% of the youngest girls said they would mind 'a lot' or 'a little' compared with 18% of the oldest girls.

Self-rated prejudice and attitudes to inter-racial marriage

In the ninth BSA report, Young (1992) found the self-rated question to be a good measure of prejudice and "a sound predictor of whether or not people display racist preferences, insofar as it clearly distinguishes between the highly prejudiced and the slightly prejudiced". The YPSA survey data were explored to see whether there were differences between those who described themselves as prejudiced, and those who did not in relation to the marriage of a relative to an Asian or black person. The two tables on the next page show findings which are in accord with those obtained by Young in 1992 and by Airey in 1984 in respect of adult respondents; that is, people who describe themselves as prejudiced are also much more likely to object to an Asian or a black person marrying into their family.

% of young respondents minding an <u>Asian</u> person marrying a relative:

Self-related prejudice

	Prejudiced (a lot or a little)		**Not prejudiced**	
	Male	**Female**	**Male**	**Female**
A lot	22	12	1	2
A little	25	30	5	4
Not mind	53	52	92	94

Whereas 47% of the boys and 42% of the girls who described themselves as 'prejudiced' stated they would mind 'a lot' or 'a little' if a relative married an Asian person, only 6% of both boys and girls who described themselves as 'not prejudiced' said they would mind either 'a lot' or 'a little'. More than nine out of 10 of the 'non-prejudiced' group stated that they had no objection to such a marriage.

The data, shown below, for a black person marrying into the respondent's family reveals that the figures are slightly lower than for Asians for the 'prejudiced' group (40% of boys and 36% of girls would mind 'a lot' or 'a little' if a relative married a black person compared to 47% and 42% respectively in respect of Asians), but the figures for the 'not prejudiced' group remain about the same as for Asians *and* much lower than for the prejudiced group.

% of young respondents minding a <u>black</u> person marrying a relative:

Self-rated prejudice

	Prejudiced (a lot or a little)		**Not prejudiced**	
	Male	**Female**	**Male**	**Female**
A lot	15	10	1	2
A little	25	26	5	3
Not mind	58	59	88	94

These results suggest that even though the 'not prejudiced' group does not differentiate between Asians and black people, the 'prejudiced' group shows a propensity to be slightly more accepting of a black person as a spouse for a relative compared with an Asian.

Attitudes of Asians to inter-racial marriages

The attitudes of young Asians to inter-racial marriages were also examined. However, the results need to be interpreted with caution, given the very small number of Asian respondents. (As only six people who identified themselves as black were interviewed, results about their attitudes to mixed race marriages are not included here.)

The results, shown in the table below, indicate that about one-third of the young Asian respondents thought that 'most' Asians would mind 'a lot' if a relative married a white person or a black person. Slightly more than half also believed that 'most' Asians would mind 'a little' if a white person married into their family, whereas slightly more than one-third thought that 'most' Asians would mind 'a little' if a black person married a relative.

Number[1] saying most Asians would mind:

	White person in family	Black person in family
A lot	10	11
A little	17	13
Not mind	4	5
Don't know/not answered	1	3

As shown in the table below, when Asian respondents were asked if they themselves would mind, they claimed, like their white peers, to be more accepting of inter-racial relationships.

Number[1] of Asian respondents saying they would mind:

	White person in family	Black person in family
A lot	1	0
A little	7	10
Not mind	22	17
Don't know/not answered	2	5

1. Actual number of respondents who selected the various options are given rather than percentages as there were only 32 respondents in the Asian sub-sample.

Only one Asian young person admitted to minding 'a lot' if a white person married into their family whereas no-one said that they would mind 'a lot' if a relative were to marry a black person. A quarter of young Asian respondents said they would either mind 'a lot' or 'a little' if a relative married a white person compared with about one-third stating that they would mind 'a little' if a black person married into their family.

Perceived discrimination in the job market

Prejudice towards Asians and black people in British society has often resulted in discrimination against them in the spheres of employment, housing and provision of services. Research carried out into the effectiveness of the 1965 Race Relations Act (Daniel, 1968) provided evidence that Asians and black people suffered widespread discrimination in all areas of their daily life.

Discrimination in employment opportunities against Asian and black people has been the subject of many reports and surveys. Brown (1984), reporting on the findings from the third Policy Studies Institute (PSI) survey, noted that the registered unemployment rates in 1982 were 13% for whites, 25% for West Indians and 20% for Asians. More than a decade later, the unemployment rates, as reported in Working Brief (Convery, 1995), once again reflect the discrimination and disadvantage encountered by Asian and black jobseekers. Compared with the overall Great Britain unemployment rate of 9.6%, the unemployment rate was 9.1% for white jobseekers, 25% for black and 18.3% for Asian jobseekers. Although the overall rate of unemployment has dropped in the last 12 years, the unemployment rate for Asian and black people has remained almost static, thus widening the gap between unemployed white people and unemployed people from these two minority ethnic groups.

Over the years, research studies have presented evidence of discrimination and surveys have tried to gauge the views of the British public on the level of discrimination they believe to be present in the job market. The third PSI survey collected just such information by asking respondents, "Do you think there are employers in Britain who would refuse a job to a person because of their race or colour?". Seventy-three per cent of white male respondents said 'yes' as did 69% of white female respondents (Brown, 1984).

The YPSA survey asked a similar question of the respondents about Asian people and a parallel question was asked about discrimination against 'people of West Indian origin' in the job market.

On the whole do you think people of Asian/West Indian origin are not given jobs these days because of their race ... a lot, a little, or hardly at all?

The results, along with those obtained when the adult respondents were asked the same questions in the 1994 BSA survey, are presented below.

Perceived discrimination in the job market against:

	Asians by:		**West Indians by:**	
	Young people	**Adults**	**Young people**	**Adults**
	%	%	%	%
A lot	17	20	16	23
A little	50	42	50	42
Hardly at all	28	32	27	28
Don't know	5	6	6	6

The percentage of young people who think there is 'a lot' of discrimination against Asians in the job market is very similar to that for West Indians. However, the percentage of adults who think there is 'a lot' of discrimination is slightly higher, especially in respect of discrimination against West Indians, and is, perhaps worryingly, close to that obtained in the first BSA survey when 20% of adult respondents thought there was 'a lot' of discrimination in employment against Asians and 25% thought so about West Indians (Airey, 1984). The unaltered perception among adults may be because of their direct experience of discrimination encountered by Asians and West Indians in the work place. Almost a third of adults think there is hardly any discrimination against Asians in the job market and slightly more than a quarter of the adults think so about West Indians. Around a quarter of the young people also believed that there was hardly any discrimination against Asians and West Indians.

Data from the YPSA survey provided evidence of gender differences in the levels of perceived discrimination against Asian and West Indian jobseekers.

Gender differences in perceived discrimination in the job market against:

	Asians by:		West Indians by:	
	Males	Females	Males	Females
	%	%	%	%
A lot	17	19	17	16
A little	47	52	48	53
Hardly at all	31	25	29	26
Don't know	6	4	6	5

Girls were more likely to perceive racial discrimination against the two minority ethnic groups as when the two levels of perceived discrimination ('a lot' and 'a little') are combined, it can be seen that 64% and 65% of boys think that there is either 'a lot' or 'a little' discrimination against Asians and West Indians, respectively, compared with 71% and 69% of girls who think that there is some level of discrimination against Asians and West Indians respectively.

When responses of white[1] youngsters were examined by political party identification, a greater percentage of Labour identifiers believed that there was 'a lot' of discrimination in the job market against both Asian and West Indian jobseekers.

Party political differences in perceived discrimination in the job market against:

	Asians by:			West Indians by:		
	Conserva -tives	Labour	Liberal Democrats	Conserva- tives	Labour	Liberal Democrats
	%	%	%	%	%	%
A lot	8	22	16	8	21	13
A little	53	50	46	54	52	46
Hardly at all	36	22	34	33	20	38
Don't know	4	5	4	5	7	4

[1]The responses of Asian and black respondents were omitted from this analysis as it was found that 21 out of 38 Asian and black respondents identified with the Labour party. Analysis showed that although this was a small number, it had an effect on the percentage obtained in respect of Labour identifiers, when all the YPSA respondents were included in the analysis.

By aggregating the figures for the two different levels of discrimination ('a lot' and 'a little'), it can be seen that Labour identifiers who think that there is some degree of discrimination against Asians (72%) and West Indians (73%) exceed the number of both Conservative (61% and 62% respectively) and Liberal Democrat (62% and 59%, respectively) identifiers. It is not surprising to note, therefore, that only about two out of 10 Labour identifiers think that there is hardly any discrimination against Asian and West Indian jobseekers compared with slightly above a third of both Conservative and Liberal Democrat identifiers.

Perceived discrimination in the judicial system

The respondents in the YPSA survey were presented with the following scenario:

> *Suppose two people — one white, one black — each appear in court, charged with a crime they did* **not** *commit. What do you think their chances are of being found* **guilty***?*

The table below compares the responses given by young people in the YPSA survey with those from adult respondents asked the same question in the BSA surveys in 1990 and 1994.

Likelihood of a black or a white person being found guilty of a crime they did not commit: comparison with adults' views in 1990 and 1994

	1990 (Adults)	1994 (Adults)	1994 (Young People)
	%	%	%
White more likely	3	4	3
Same chance	49	49	48
Black more likely	42	44	44

Source: 1990 and 1994: BSA surveys.

In 1994, 44% of both young people and adults interviewed thought that a black person was more likely to be found guilty, indicating that young people are as likely to believe that the judicial system discriminates against black people as adults. Only around one-half of those interviewed — adults and young people alike — held the belief that the judicial system treats everyone equally.

Their views can be compared with the finding reported in the Runnymede Bulletin (Runnymede Trust, 1995) that 25% of people stopped and searched in 1993 were black. This percentage far exceeds the 1.1% of black people over 16 (those of African-Caribbean, Indian and Pakistani origin) residing in Britain, as reported in Social Trends (1995).

The data were then examined for race and gender differences. White girls were found to be slightly more sceptical than boys about the fairness of the judicial system where a black person was concerned, as were the Asian and black respondents (the data for black and Asian respondents have been combined because of the small numbers interviewed in the survey).

Likelihood of being found guilty: race and gender differences in the young respondents' attitudes to the judicial system

	White			**Asian and black**		
	All	**Male**	**Female**	**All**	**Male**	**Female**
	%	%	%			
White more likely	3	3	2	(3)	(1)	(2)
Same chance	50	51	49	(12)	(7)	(5)
Black more likely	42	40	44	(23)	(9)	(14)

Actual numbers rather than percentages for Asian and black respondents are presented in brackets as the sample size for this sub-group of respondents was very small (17 males and 21 females).

More than half of all Asian and black respondents as opposed to about four in 10 of all white respondents believed that an innocent black person was more likely to be found guilty. Only a quarter of Asian and black girls believed that the law is dispensed in a fair and equitable manner compared with slightly less than half (7 out of 17) of Asian and black young men and about half of both white young men and young women.

Examination of age and gender differences in the responses of white respondents in the YPSA survey revealed an interesting pattern. (The responses of black and Asian respondents have been omitted from this table to provide a clearer focus on the views of the white respondents.)

Likelihood of being found guilty: age and gender differences in white respondents' attitudes to the judicial system

	Male			Female		
	12–15	**16–17**	**18–19**	**12–15**	**16–17**	**18–19**
	%	%	%	%	%	%
White more likely	4	2	3	2	3	3
Same Chance	46	59	58	48	52	44
Black more likely	42	36	33	45	40	48

One-third of the boys in the oldest age group thought that a black person was more likely to be found guilty compared with about one-half of the girls in the same age group. Moreover, a greater number of the 16–19-year-old boys appear to think that the judicial system is colour-blind compared with 12–15-year-old boys. Interestingly, fewer of the girls in the oldest age group appear to believe in the fairness of the legal system compared with 12–17-year-old girls. One inference which can be drawn from these findings is that older girls are perhaps more aware of racial discrimination in the judicial system than boys in the same age group.

Views on anti-discrimination legislation

Prejudice cannot be legislated against, hence the 1976 Race Relations Act, which came into force in the middle of 1977, was created to legislate against direct and indirect discrimination — its behavioural concomitant — by making it unlawful to discriminate against someone on the basis of their colour, race, nationality or national or ethnic origins, in the arenas of employment, housing, education and the provision of goods, facilities and services. The 1976 Act also set up the Commission for Racial Equality to enforce the law and to support those subjected to racial discrimination (Carmichael, 1982; Gordon and Newnham, 1986).

Given that the Race Relations Act has been in force for almost two decades, the question arises about whether young people who have not only grown up in a multi-racial Britain but have had exposure to incidents of racial discrimination against Asian and black people, via the media, are more in favour of anti-discrimination legislation than the adults. The table below compares the results from the YPSA survey with those from the adult BSA survey conducted in 1994 and in previous years to the question:

> *There is a law in Britain* **against** *racial discrimination, that is against giving unfair preference to a particular race in housing, jobs and so on. Do you generally* **support** *or* **oppose** *the idea of a law for this purpose?*

Attitudes of young people and adults to anti-discrimination legislation

	Adults					Young people
	1986	**1989**	**1990**	**1991**	**1994**	**1994**
	%	%	%	%	%	%
Support the legislation	65	68	68	76	73	75

Source: 1986 to 1994: BSA surveys.

Most adults and young people appear to support anti-discrimination legislation. It should be noted that 11% of the young people responded with a 'don't know' or did not answer the question compared with only 5% of the adults.

In terms of party identification, support for anti-discrimination legislation was found to be greatest among Liberal Democrat identifiers (89%) compared with Labour identifiers (78%), with Conservatives lagging slightly behind. Surprisingly, the opposition to the legislation was greatest among Labour identifiers (14%) compared with Liberal Democrats (7%), with Conservatives (12%) just behind Labour identifiers.

Views on racial prejudice in five years' time

Previous BSA surveys have tried to elicit views on the extent of racial prejudice in the future. As the table below shows, there was an increase in the level of optimism from 1986 to 1991, with optimists outnumbering pessimists in 1991. The YPSA survey also included the question on the future of racial prejudice in Britain and the young people's responses are presented alongside those of adults asked this question over the years.

Do you think there will be **more, less** *or* **about the same** *amount of racial prejudice in Britain in five years time compared with now?*

% who think that racial prejudice in Britain will be:

	Adults						Young people
	1986	**1987**	**1989**	**1990**	**1991**	**1994**	**1994**
More in five years' time	46	46	32	37	21	39	25
Less	13	12	19	20	25	20	35
About the same	36	37	45	39	50	35	36

Source: 1986 to 1994: BSA surveys.

The figures for 1994 indicate that the optimists among the young outnumber the pessimists as 35% think there will be less racial prejudice in five years' time compared with 25% who think there will be more. However, of the adults interviewed for the survey in 1994, pessimists not only outnumber optimists but have increased about twofold since 1991, with 39% thinking that there will be more racial prejudice in five years' time.

Gender and age differences were explored next in young people's responses and the results are shown in the table below.

Gender and age differences — racial prejudice in Britain will be:

	Male			Female		
	12–15	**16–17**	**18–19**	**12–15**	**16–17**	**18–19**
	%	%	%	%	%	%
More in five years' time	23	18	33	28	27	22
Less	38	43	30	31	37	32
About the same	36	38	33	37	33	42

In the three age groups for girls and the first two age groups for boys, optimists exceed pessimists. However, the degree of optimism varies for boys and girls. Boys aged 16 to 17 appear to be most optimistic, with 43% thinking that there will be less racial prejudice in five years' time compared with 18% who think there will be more. Girls aged 12 to 15 years, on the other hand, appear to be least optimistic with only three percentage points between optimists and pessimists, in the favour of optimists.

Interestingly, or perhaps not, given some of the earlier findings in respect of 18–19-year-old boys, this group alone out of the six groups (shown in the table above), is more pessimistic than optimistic, with 3% more thinking that there will be more racial prejudice in five years' time. By contrast, fewer girls in the 18–19 age band appear to think that there will be more racial prejudice in five years' time compared with girls in the other age groups. The opinion about racial discrimination remaining at the present levels in five years' time varies within the three age groups for both boys and girls. It ranges from one-third of 16–17-year-old girls and the oldest boys holding this view, to 42% of the oldest girls believing it to be the case.

The data were then analysed to look for differences between those identifying with the three main political parties and the results are shown in the next table.

Party political differences — racial prejudice in Britain will be:

	Conservative	**Labour**	**Liberal Democrats**
	%	%	%
More in five years' time	29	27	20
Less	49	30	34
About the same	21	39	45

The young people identifying with the three political parties appear to be more optimistic than pessimistic about the future. However, an interesting paradox emerges. Although, on the one hand, more Conservative identifiers think that racial prejudice will increase in five years' time compared with Labour or Liberal Democrat identifiers, the data also suggest that many more Conservatives (about one-half) also think that there will be less racial prejudice in future. Moreover, not only are there fewest pessimists among the Liberal Democrats, with only 20% thinking that there will be more racial prejudice in future, this group also has the highest number who believe that the situation is likely to remain the same. Future YPSA surveys will be in a better position to shed light on this conundrum.

Views on the importance of race in doing well in life

The YPSA survey included a question to gauge the opinions of young people on the importance they attach to 'race' in getting ahead in life. The young respondents were asked a series of questions about doing well in life. One question asked:

How important is a person's race?

The overall response showed that 2% thought it was 'essential', 9% thought it was 'very important' and 15% thought it was 'fairly important'. Seventy-two per cent thought that it was either 'not very important' or 'not at all important'.

Age and gender differences were explored next and the results are shown below.

Age and gender differences in views on the importance of race in doing well in life

	Male			Female		
	12–15	**16–17**	**18–19**	**12–15**	**16–17**	**18–19**
	%	%	%	%	%	%
Essential	2	3	3	1	0	0
Very important	9	6	3	10	11	9
Fairly important	16	18	18	11	20	10
Not very important	39	41	52	36	34	45
Not at all important	32	29	21	37	33	32

Very few respondents regarded a person's race as 'essential' to their future success. About one in 10 of the girls in all three age groups and of the youngest boys regarded it as 'very important'. If the figures for 'essential', 'very important' and 'fairly important' are aggregated it appears that although 31% of the 16–17-year-old girls believe a person's race to be either 'very' or 'fairly important', only 19% of the oldest girls believe this to be the case. About a quarter of the oldest boys believe that a person's race has some part to play in securing a person's future success whereas slightly more of the boys aged 12 to 17 years believe this. About half of the oldest boys believe that race is 'not very important' compared with 45% of girls in the same age band. If figures are aggregated for 'not very important' and 'not at all important' it can be seen that more than three-quarters of the oldest girls attach little or no importance to a person's race compared with 67% of girls aged 16 to 17 years.

Evidence was sought for the influence of political party identity on the views of young people on this issue. The findings revealed that young people who identify with Liberal Democrats and Conservatives appear to attach less importance to a person's race. Only 16% of Liberal Democrats and 22% of Conservatives think that race is either 'essential', 'very important' or 'fairly important' compared with a third of Labour identifiers.

Party political differences in views on the importance of race in doing well in life

	Conservative	Labour	Liberal Democrats
	%	%	%
Essential	2	1	0
Very important	6	13	5
Fairly important	14	19	11
Not very important	41	37	48
Not at all important	35	27	36

These results also show that 84% of Liberal Democrats think that a person's race is 'not very' or 'not at all' important in ensuring their future success, compared with around three-quarters of Conservatives and 64% of Labour identifiers.

When YPSA data were grouped by racial origin, the responses of Asian and black young people were combined, because of the small numbers. Although 24% of white respondents stated that a person's race was of some importance, from 'essential' through to 'fairly important', half of the Asian and black young people believed it to be either 'very' or 'fairly important'. These results seem to suggest that the young people (19 out of 38) from these two minority ethnic groups believe that their chances of future success are determined by their racial background.

Degree of agreement between the attitudes of the young people on prejudice and discrimination with the attitudes of the adults

A number of questions asked of young respondents were also asked of adults in the BSA survey, providing an ideal opportunity to compare the views and attitudes of the young people with those of the adults, and to look for degrees of concurrence between their views. It should be noted at this stage that the comparisons which follow were carried out between young people and their adult relatives who were interviewed for the adult BSA survey. The adult relative could have been a parent or an older sibling, although in the vast majority of cases, the adult relative was a parent. As the adult BSA survey allocated respondents to one of the three versions of the questionnaire, not all questions were asked of all the adult relatives of YPSA respondents. Consequently, comparisons could only be made between those YPSA and BSA respondents where the relevant question was asked of both.

Given the nature of comparisons carried out, actual values rather than percentages have been provided. The young people's levels of perceived prejudice against Asian and black people were compared first with adults' perceived prejudice levels and are presented in the next table.[1]

Prejudice against Asian and black people

Views of parents of YPSA respondents

	Prejudice against Asian people				**Prejudice against black people**			
	A lot	**A little**	**Hardly any**	**Total young people**	**A lot**	**A little**	**Hardly any**	**Total young people**
Young people's views:								
A lot	**119**	53	9	**181**	**71**	66	9	**146**
A little	89	**71**	8	**168**	86	**79**	16	**181**
Hardly any	14	8	**1**	**23**	17	19	**5**	**41**
Total no. of adults	222	132	18	372	174	164	30	368

The results show that 222 adult respondents thought there was 'a lot' of prejudice against Asians. Slightly more than half of the young respondents agreed with them. Of the 132 adults who thought there was a little prejudice against Asians, again slightly more than half of the young people residing in the same households agreed with them. Of the 18 adults who thought there was hardly any prejudice against Asians, only one young person was in agreement with his/her adult relative. Overall, more young people thought that there is either a little prejudice or hardly any prejudice against Asians

[1]The figures in the following three tables represent not only the number of parents who gave a particular response as indicated by the column heading, *but* also the number of young people who gave a particular response as indicated by the row heading.

and fewer that there is 'a lot' of prejudice compared with adults. As only 191 (out of 372) young people agreed with the adults in their households, the degree of concurrence is 51%, that is, 51% of the young people interviewed agreed with their adult relatives about the degree of prejudice against Asians.

The results with regard to agreement between adults and young people on the degree of prejudice against black people are essentially the same, with one main difference. As only 155 (out of 368) young people concurred with adults on this issue, the degree of concurrence is 42%, that is, around 42% of young people agree with their adult relatives on the degree and extent of prejudice against black people.

Comparison between self-rated levels of prejudice — young people and adult relatives

The next table shows a comparison between adults' and young people's self-rated levels of prejudice against people of other races.

	Adults' self-rated prejudice			
Young people's self-rated prejudice	**Very prejudiced**	**A little**	**Not prejudiced**	**Total young people**
Very prejudiced	**0**	3	3	**6**
A little prejudiced	7	**46**	39	**92**
Not prejudiced	1	72	**199**	**272**
Total no. of adults	8	121	241	370

The degree of concurrence between the young people who admitted to the same level of prejudice as their adult relatives was 66% (245 out of 370). The table also shows that more young people claim to be prejudice-free compared with the adult respondents in their household.

Comparison between views on anti-discriminatory legislation — young people and adult relatives

The last comparison was carried out to look at the degree of concurrence between young people and their adult relatives in their support for anti-discrimination legislation.

	Adults		
Young people	**Support**	**Oppose**	**Total young people**
Support	**223**	57	280
Oppose	38	**17**	55
Total no. of adults	261	74	335

There appears to be a very high degree of agreement between adults and young people on this issue. Of the young people, 72% (240 out of 335) agree with their adult relatives on the need for legislation against racial discrimination, although slightly more young people claim to support the law compared with adults.

Conclusion

The data from the *Young People's Social Attitudes Survey* has provided a rich array of findings about young people's views and attitudes on racial prejudice and racial discrimination. On the whole, young people appear to be very aware of prejudice against Asian and black people in British society, and of discrimination against them in the employment sector and in the judicial system. They also admit to lower levels of prejudice than adults.

The young people appear to be supportive of anti-discrimination legislation, are more optimistic than adults about a lessening of racial prejudice in five years' time and believe that race is not that important a factor in a person's future success.

Girls appear to be more aware and perhaps more sensitive about racial discrimination against Asians and black people and claim lower levels of prejudice than boys.

A surprising finding of the YPSA survey is that 16–19-year-old boys are more likely to believe in the fairness of the judicial system than 12–15-year-old boys. Surprising, too, are the findings that 16–17-year-old boys admit to being more prejudiced than younger or older boys and that 18–19-year-old boys are more pessimistic about racial prejudice in future compared with younger boys, who are much more optimistic.

On balance, young people appear to be more liberal and much less prejudiced than adults. If we are to believe in the oft-quoted aphorism that the youth of today holds the future of Britain in its hands, then this belief can perhaps be extended to the hope that they may also hold the key to racial harmony in multi-racial Britain as it moves towards the twenty-first century. It is perhaps not too futile a hope, given the egalitarian views and attitudes disclosed by young people interviewed in the 1994 YPSA survey.

References

Airey, C. (1984), 'Social and Moral Values', in Jowell, R. and Airey, C. (eds), *British Social Attitudes: the 1984 report*, Aldershot: Gower.

Armstrong, B. (ed.) (1989), *A People without Prejudice? The Experience of Racism in Scotland*, London: The Runnymede Trust.

Bagley, C. and Verma, G.K. (1979), *Racial Prejudice, the Individual and Society*, Hampshire: Saxon House, Teakfield Ltd.

Bethlehem, D.W. (1985), *A Social Psychology of Prejudice*, London: Croom Helm.

Brown, C. (1984), *Black and White Britain: The Third PSI Survey*, London: Heinemann.

Carmichael, C. (1982), *Race in Britain. An Information Pack*, London: Council for Voluntary Service.

Central Statistical Office (1995), *Social Trends*, London: HMSO.

Convery, P. (1995), 'Labour Force survey shows Jobs Growth', *Working Brief*, 61, Unemployment Unit and Youthaid.

Daily Express, August 9, 1995, *Two thirds of us would say yes to mixed marriages*, p.8.

Daniel, W.W. (1968), *Racial Discrimination in England*, Harmondsworth: Penguin.

Davey, A. (1983), *Learning to be Prejudiced: growing up in multi-ethnic Britain*, London: Edward Arnold.

Gordon, P. and Newnham, A. (1986), *Different worlds: Racism and Discrimination in Britain*, 2nd edn, London: Runnymede Trust.

Jones, T. (1993), *Britain's Ethnic Minorities*, London: Policy Studies Institute.

Modood, T. (1994), *Racial Equality: Colour, Culture and Justice*, London: Institute for Public Policy Research.

Pilkington, A. (1984), *Race Relations in Britain*, London: University Tutorial Press Ltd.

Reeves, F. (1982), *The Concept of Prejudice: An Evaluative Review*, Working papers on Ethnic Relations, No. 17, SSRC.

Runnymede Trust (1995), 'Policing Update', *The Runnymede Bulletin*, no. 287, July/August.

Smith, D.J. (1976), *The Facts of Racial Disadvantage*, Political and Economic Planning, Vol XLII, Broadsheet no. 560, London: PEP.

Solomos, J. (1989), *Race and Racism in Contemporary Britain*, Macmillan Education Ltd.

Young, K. (1992), 'Class, Race and Opportunity', in Jowell, R., Brook, L., Prior, G. and Taylor, B. (eds), *British Social Attitudes: the 9th Report*, Aldershot: Dartmouth.

4 Young people, crime, justice and punishment

DIANA McNEISH

Most debate around youth and crime focuses on young people as perpetrators. Much less is said about young people as victims of crime and even less about the attitudes of young people towards criminal behaviour and their views on how offenders should be dealt with. The public image of youth as a social problem is mirrored in the majority of studies which have tended to concentrate on the minority of young people whose behaviour is outside social norms. A disinterested observer reviewing the literature on young people could easily conclude that youth is a pathological condition. As Hudson points out, the creation of adolescence, that "uneasy space between childhood and adulthood", has proved a rich seam for social science (Hudson, 1987: 131–2).

No seam has proved richer than that concerned with young people who break the law. The language may have changed from juvenile delinquency to youth justice, but the issues for those who study it remain fairly constant. There exists a wealth of material on the incidence and causes of youth crime and the responses to it but most of this literature has been written from an adult perspective. Comparatively little has been written from the perspective of young people. This chapter summarizes the findings of the *Young People's Social Attitudes* (YPSA) *Survey* in relation to crime and justice. It encompasses young people's fear of crime, their experiences of it and their views on the appropriate response to offenders.

Most people have images of likely perpetrators of crime, and young people, specifically young men, feature quite strongly in such images. Pearson (1983), Cohen (1980) and others have documented adult fears of young people and crime throughout history, providing ample illustration of how each generation of adults tends to believe that the youth of the day has less respect for the law than ever before. The sentiments expressed by the following extract from the Leeds Mercury, February 1869 are doubtless similar to those felt by many adults today:

> *"It will be admitted without controversy, I think, that juvenile crime must have largely increased with the rapid and unprecedented increase in the many fatal agencies which have been put in motion seeking the*

demoralisation and destruction of our youth such as casinos, singing saloons and cheap concert halls, the extraordinary facilities for drinking and betting."

The struggle to understand crime and to find ways of dealing with it has a long and chequered history. Nowhere has this been more visible than in the history of juvenile justice policy which has highlighted fundamental questions about both the nature of crime and the nature of childhood and adolescence.

Youth justice policy

Youth justice policy can be seen to reflect prevailing judgments on a number of questions. Can young people be held morally responsible for their behaviour and, if so, at what age? What makes a young person become delinquent — their upbringing? their environment? their peer group? their situation in relation to the class struggle? their masculinity? their genes? How should young people who offend be dealt with — by punishment or with welfare? These questions have spawned numerous arguments and counter-arguments based on evidence from studies which have sought to identify the causes and correlates of crime. These have been usefully summarized by a number of writers (Rutter and Giller, 1983; Downes and Rock, 1988; Tarling, 1993).

Such questions can be traced through the changes in the law relating to young people and crime. Until the mid-nineteenth century, the law treated children similarly to adults and frequently meted out similarly harsh punishments:

> *"On one day alone in February 1814 at the Old Bailey sessions five children were condemned to death: Fowler aged 12 and Wolfe aged 12 for burglary in a dwelling; Morris aged 8, Solomons aged 9 and Burrell aged 11 for burglary and stealing a pair of shoes."*
>
> (Muncie, 1984: 33)

From the implementation of the 1837 Parkhurst Act, which began the segregation of adult and child prisoners, we can see the beginning of a shift in adult attitudes towards young offenders. Victorian philanthropists, such as Thomas Barnardo, promoted the view of children as the innocent victims of deprivation and depravity — to be saved rather than punished. Notions of welfare and punishment have jostled for position throughout the twentieth century, underlining adult uncertainty not only about the most effective ways of dealing with the problem of youth but also about the very nature of youth. If the number of legal changes can be used as an indicator, then adult uncertainty has reached a peak over the past 15 years. Since 1980 there have been numerous changes in the law affecting the treatment of young people who offend.

Amidst this uncertainty, we continue to struggle with the same questions. The law remains ambivalent about young people's moral responsibility and their ability to understand right and wrong. Under current law the principle of *doli incapax* still applies, whereby children under the age of 10 are deemed not to be responsible for any criminal offence and up to the age of 14 it is incumbent upon the prosecution to demonstrate not only that the young person knew what they did was wrong but they knew that it was seriously wrong (not just naughty or mischievous). This is a concrete demonstration of the belief that children are basically innocent. This belief gets shaken periodically by an event of abnormal horror. The murder of James Bulger by two ten-year-olds brought out a sharply contrasting belief — that children are capable of evil. It is this belief that appears to have dominated the recent policy agenda. Much has been made of the small number of young people who commit a disproportionate amount of crime and there has been an image of a society under siege from these persistent young offenders with media vilification of individual young people dubbed with names like 'Ratboy'. The move over the past few years has clearly been away from welfare towards a more punitive approach. The introduction of Secure Training Centres for young people is one example of this, the debate about 'boot camps' another.

The level of political and media attention paid to the problem of young offenders in recent years has led some observers to refer to a new 'moral panic' about youth crime, the 'scare in the community' (Pitts, 1995). Within this context, there has been comparatively little attention paid to the majority of young people who do not commit crime or the views of young people themselves, both those who offend and those who do not.

In the YPSA survey, young people were asked about their experiences of crime as victims, their worries about crime and the steps they take to avoid it. They were also asked for their views on the fairness of the justice system, on ways of preventing crime and how young offenders should be dealt with. Finally, they were asked for their views on the death penalty.

Young people's experiences and fear of crime

The YPSA survey reveals that a majority of young people (82%) have been the victim of crime. This will sometimes be a crime committed in their household, and sometimes a crime specifically directed towards them. A particularly worrying number of young people had been physically attacked or threatened — cause for concern, even allowing for respondent bias in the interpretation of the question (we have no way of assessing the seriousness of incidents).

The incidence of young people as victims of crime was noted by Hartless *et al.* (1995) in their surveys of 11–15-year-olds in Glasgow and Edinburgh. Using a much wider range of examples of victimization than in the present survey (including being stared at in the street, bullied and followed) Hartless *et al.* found that 82% of young people had experienced at least one such incident in the past year with only 10% of the respondents never having been victimized. Of their sample, 51% had been threatened at some time during their life.

The findings of the YPSA survey suggest that the majority of young people are very aware of crime. Sixty-two per cent of young people worry about crime and 94% take some measures to avoid it. On the other hand, the majority of young people (57%) feel either very or fairly safe when walking around in their area after dark. Previous surveys have found that young people express a fear of crime. Furnham and Gunter (1989), for instance, found that around half of their respondents worried at least sometimes that they themselves or someone they lived with might be the victim of crime. Data from *Social Trends* show that the fear of crime tends to be slightly higher in the 16–29 age group than for older age groups for particular crimes such as car theft, and markedly higher for rape (HMSO, 1995a: 159).

The following summarizes the main findings of the YPSA survey on young people as crime victims and their worries about crime.

Young people as victims of crime

The majority of young people (82%) in the survey had experience of crime as a victim. The table below shows their experiences.

Eighty-eight per cent of young people said they personally knew victims of crime.

Experience of crime as a victim

Have you yourself ever...

	% saying yes
... been physically attacked?	16
... been threatened?	33
... had your home burgled?	18
... had a car belonging to you or your family stolen or things stolen from it?	45
... had your home or car damaged by vandals?	39
... had your bike stolen or damaged by vandals?	24
... had something else stolen?	31

Effect of these experiences on awareness and fear of crime

- Of those who had been a victim of crime, 66% said that this had made them more aware of crime; 33% said that it had made no difference.
- Of those young people who had become more aware as a result of being a victim of crime, 40% said their experience of crime had made them more afraid whereas 58% said they had not become more afraid.
- Of those young people who personally knew a victim of crime, 68% said that as a consequence they had become more aware of crime; 31% said that it had made no difference.
- Forty-six per cent of those who had become more aware of crime as a result of personally knowing a victim of crime said that this had made them more afraid of crime.

It would seem that the experience of being a victim of crime or knowing someone who has been a victim does raise young people's awareness, but not necessarily their fear, of crime. However, we have no way of knowing from the data how serious the crimes were or the extent to which some young people had been victims on more than one occasion.

Young people's worries about crime

The table below shows the responses of young people to questions about worries about crime: 62% of young people said they worried about the possibility of they themselves or someone they lived with becoming the victim of crime; 38% said they did not.

Worries about crime

Do you ever worry about the possibility that you or anyone else who lives with you might be the victim of crime?

	%
Yes	62
No	38
If yes, is this …	
… a big worry	10
… a bit of a worry	35
… an occasional doubt	16

How safe do you feel walking alone in this area after dark?

	%
Very safe	14
Fairly safe	43
A bit unsafe	28
Very unsafe	8
Never walk alone	6

What may surprise many people is the relatively small number of young people who feel very unsafe. Indeed, 57% of young people say they feel very or fairly safe in their area after dark.

Measures taken to avoid crime

Young people were asked what they did to avoid crime and their responses, shown in the following table, suggest that the majority exercise a good degree of caution in an attempt to avoid crime. Only 6% of young people said that they did nothing to avoid crime.

Over 70% of young people say they are careful to lock their homes and cars and over half avoid going to certain places. Only a few young people said they avoided public transport or carried a personal alarm or weapon. The responses suggest a population of young people who are conscious of the need to take measures to avoid crime but not unduly alarmed.

Measures taken to avoid crime

Here are some things that some people do to avoid crime. Which of these do you do?

	%
I am careful to lock up our home (and/or car)	72
I don't go out alone	20
I don't answer the door	11
I avoid going out at certain times	33
I avoid going to certain places	53
I carry a personal alarm or a weapon	6
I avoid public transport	6
I make sure other people in the family take precautions	20
None	6

Gender differences in experiences of crime

There can be little doubt that gender is a key variable in the consideration of crime. As Coote points out, there seems to exist 'a destructive cycle in which young men are not only the main perpetrators but also the main victims of crime' (Coote 1994: 4).

The majority of studies into the experiences and fear of crime note marked gender differences. The 1992 *British Crime Survey* (HMSO, 1993) reveals that 53% of victims of street crime are young males whereas young females account for just 14% of victims. Criminal statistics also show that males aged between 16 and 29 are twice as likely to become a homicide victim than females of the same age group. (In 1992 there were 118 male homicides in 16–29 age group compared with 56 females; HMSO, 1992.) These factors are not reflected in the fears expressed by young men. Among young people, Furnham and Gunter's (1989) survey also found that although 74% of males felt safe walking alone after dark, this was true of only 37% of females.

This YPSA survey shows males representing the highest proportion of young people who said they had been attacked or threatened. For other offences, males and females reported in approximately equal numbers, with the exception of theft or damage to a bike, which was predominantly reported by males. Despite these experiences, males were no more likely than females to say that they were more aware of crime and slightly less likely to say that their experience of crime had made them more afraid. Females were slightly more likely to take measures to avoid crime, particularly crimes against the person and were significantly more likely to avoid going out alone. A much higher proportion of females than males said they felt unsafe when walking alone in their area after dark.

Males and females as victims of crime

More males (86%) than females (78%) in the survey had been the victim of crime. For most offences, there were no significant gender differences between those who said they had been victims. However, significantly more young males said they had been attacked or threatened than females. Over a quarter (26%) of males said they had been the victim of a physical attack compared with 8% of females. More young people said they had been threatened and again, there were significant gender differences, with 44% of males in the sample saying they had been threatened compared with 21% of females.

Another crime which males in the survey had more frequently experienced was theft of or damage to a bike. Of males in the sample, 34% said they had been the victim of this crime compared with 14% of females. This may be a reflection of gender differences in leisure pursuits.

Gender differences in awareness and fear of crime

Males and females were equally likely to be more aware of crime as a result of being a victim. Females reported being slightly more afraid of crime as a result of their experiences than males. Of females in the sample, 25% reported being more afraid of crime as a result of being a victim compared with 19% of males.

An equal percentage of males and females reported knowing personally someone who had been the victim of crime and there were only slight gender differences between those who said they were more aware of crime because of this (63% of females and 57% of males). More females said they felt more afraid of crime as a result of knowing a victim (35% of females compared with 20% of males).

Slightly more females than males said they worried about crime, and that it was a big worry (see following table).

The differences in general worries about crime increased with age — although males and females in the 12–15 age group were equally likely to say they worried about crime (35% and 35% respectively), in the 18–19 age group, considerably more females than males said they worried (14% compared to 7%).

Gender differences in worries about crime

Do you ever worry about the possibility that you or anyone else who lives with you might be the victim of crime?

	Males	Females
	%	%
Yes	56	67
No	44	33
If yes, is this ...		
... a big worry	8	12
... a bit of a worry	31	39
... occasional doubt	17	16

The gender differences in fear of crime are most apparent in the responses to the question about walking alone in their area after dark. Although 71% of males feel very or fairly safe walking alone in their area after dark, this is true of just 42% of females and far more females than males say they never walk alone after dark.

How safe do you feel walking alone in this area after dark?

	Males	Females
	%	%
Very safe	22	5
Fairly safe	49	37
A bit unsafe	22	36
Very unsafe	4	11
Never walk alone	2	10

Gender differences in measures taken to avoid crime

The vast majority of young people (93%) said they took some measures to avoid crime. An examination of the data for gender differences, shown in the table, suggests that females are more likely to apply crime avoidance measures than males and, in particular, are more likely to take those aimed at personal safety.

Gender differences in measures taken to avoid crime

Which of these do you do?

	Males	**Females**
	%	%
I am careful to lock up home/car	67	76
I don't go out alone	12	30
I don't answer door	7	16
I avoid going out at certain times	31	37
I avoid going to certain places	51	56
I avoid public transport	5	8
I carry an alarm or weapon	4	7
I make family take precautions	19	21
None	7	5

Age differences in experiences of crime

For the young people in this survey, there are few differences between the age groups in their experiences and fears of crime. Those differences that do emerge can be explained in terms of the activities more commonly undertaken at particular ages — one would expect older young people to be going out more and be more susceptible to attack or threat whereas younger people may be more likely to be supervised. It might have been expected that the younger age group would be more cautious in particular ways (such as being exhorted by parents not to open the door, etc.) but this does not appear to be the case.

Victims of crime by age group

There are only slight age group differences between those who said they had been a victim of crime. Those aged 12–15, those aged 16–17 and those aged 18–19 were about equally likely to report being a victim of a property-related crime. However, the proportion of young people who reported being the victim of an attack or threat went up by age group. Of those aged 18–19, 25% said they had been physically attacked, compared with 22% of 16–17-year-olds and 12% of 12–15-year-olds. Of 18–19-year-olds, 41% said they had been threatened, compared with 40% of 16–17-year-olds and 28% of 12–15-year-olds. A slightly higher proportion of young people over 16 reported knowing someone who had been the victim of crime.

Awareness and fear of crime by age group

There were no significant age group differences in the level of awareness or fear of crime as a consequence of personal experience or knowing someone who had been a victim of crime, though awareness increased slightly and fear decreased slightly with age. Young people in the older age group more commonly reported being worried about themselves or someone they lived with being the victim of crime (73% of 18–19-year-olds, 65% of 16–17-year-olds, 58% of 12–15-year-olds). In response to the question of feeling safe when walking alone in their area after dark, there were few differences between the age groups: 18–19-year-olds more commonly said they felt very safe (21% compared with 12% of 16–17-year-olds and 13% of 12–15-year-olds). Not surprisingly more younger people said they never walked out alone after dark (8% compared with 2% of 16–17-year-olds and 4% of 18–19-year-olds). There were no significant differences between age groups in the measures taken to avoid crime.

Socio-economic differences in experiences of crime

The data from the YPSA survey show few variations in the experiences and fear of crime by socio-economic group (see table). The percentage of young people who said they had been the victim of at least one of the listed crimes ranged from 79% of those in socio-economic group 4 (skilled manual) to 83% of those in socio-economic groups 1 (professional/managerial and intermediate non-manual) and 5 (semi-skilled/unskilled manual).

% of crime victims by socio-economic group

	Group			
	1	**3**	**4**	**5**
Physical attack	16	14	21	16
Threat	29	33	41	33
Burglary	14	15	21	21
Car theft	46	50	31	47
Vandalism	38	35	36	43
Bike stolen	22	23	29	20
Other item stolen	27	32	36	27

Group 1 (professional/ managerial) and Group 2 (intermediate non-manual) were combined into Group 1 for the purposes of analysis as the numbers in 2 were very small. Group 3 (junior non-manual); Group 4 (skilled manual); and Group 5 (semi-skilled and unskilled manual) are also shown.

The proportion of young people who said they personally knew a victim of crime ranged from 90% of those in the professional group to 81% of those in the semi/unskilled manual group. The proportion of those who said they worried about becoming a victim of crime rose slightly from 61% of those in group 1 to 65% of those in group 5.

Although there are no strong differences between the socio-economic groups in the measures taken to avoid crime, there are slight differences in the number of young people who say they feel safe in their area after dark. Of the young people in socio-economic group 1 (professional/managerial and intermediate non-manual), 63% said they felt very or fairly safe compared with 59% of junior non-manual, 50% of skilled manual and 54% of semi/unskilled manual; this is presumably a reflection of the neighbourhoods in which young people live.

Young people's attitudes to the fairness of the justice system

Section 95 of the 1991 Criminal Justice Act stipulates that 'persons engaged in the administration of criminal justice' have a 'duty to avoid discriminating against any person on the grounds of race or sex or any other improper ground'. Figures cited by NACRO (1991) show that, in 1989, 16% of the prison population was made up of ethnic minorities, which constitute less than 5% of the general population. The proportion of female prisoners from ethnic minorities was even greater, at 24%. Home Office figures published annually since 1985 show that ethnic minority prisoners have on average fewer previous convictions than white prisoners. Studies by Fitzgerald (1993) and others have highlighted the lesser likelihood of black defendants receiving bail before conviction for comparable offences. Given the evidence from these studies and the number of well-publicized miscarriages of justice over recent years, a reduction in faith in the fairness of the system might be predicted.

Furnham and Gunter's survey presented young people with a series of statements concerning the justice system. The extent to which young people agreed or disagreed with these statements is revealing about the degree of faith held in justice. Presented with the statement: 'It is rare for an innocent man to be wrongly sent to jail', 46% agreed and 27% disagreed; 28% agreed and 41% disagreed with the statement: 'It is often impossible for a person to get a fair trial in the UK'. However, to the statement: 'Judges and courts do not give fair and equal treatment to everyone in this country', 58% agreed, and just 14% disagreed (Furnham and Gunter, 1989: 54–5).

A study carried out in Kirklees in which young people were asked for their views on the statement: 'People get treated fairly in Court' found that 24% agreed and 39% disagreed (Brown, 1992: 7).

This general scepticism about the fairness of the British justice system is reflected in the findings of the YPSA survey which suggest that large numbers of young people view the system as unfair and discriminatory. Interestingly, from the responses to the scenarios they were given, young people appear to perceive a greater degree of discrimination on the grounds of poverty compared with race, with being Irish seen as less of a difficulty. The survey also suggests that scepticism about the fairness of the justice system sets in at quite an early age. One might expect a greater level of cynicism among the older age group but this does not appear to be the case. That British justice should be viewed as unfair by such a high proportion of 12–15-year-olds is cause for concern.

Young people in our survey were presented with the scenario of two people each appearing in court charged with an offence they did not commit. The type of offence was not specified. In one case, one of the defendants was black, the other white; in a second case, one of the defendants was poor, the other rich; in a third case, one of the defendants was Irish, the other British. Young people were asked in each case what they thought the chances were of the defendants being found guilty.

- Forty-eight per cent of respondents thought that a white and a black person would have the same chance of being found guilty, whereas 44% thought that the black person was more likely to be found guilty.
- Thirty per cent thought that a rich and a poor person would have the same chance of being found guilty, whereas 64% thought that a poor person was more likely to be found guilty.
- Sixty-seven per cent thought that a British and an Irish person would have the same chance of being found guilty; 26% thought the Irish person was more likely to be found guilty.

Gender, age and socio-economic differences in attitudes towards justice

The data seem to suggest similar levels of scepticism between young females and males.

- Females were slightly more likely to see the justice system as unfair on the grounds of race: 47% of females thought a black person was more likely to be found guilty compared with 41% of males.

- Young males were slightly more likely to see the justice system as unfair on the grounds of poverty: 62% of females thought a poor person more likely to be found guilty compared with 67% of males.
- Males and females were about equally likely to see injustice on the grounds of being Irish: 25% of females thought an Irish person more likely to be found guilty compared with 28% of males.

The data also suggest few differences in attitudes between age groups. Of the 12–15 age group, 45% thought a black person was more likely to be found guilty compared with 42% of the 16–17 age group and 43% of the 18–19 age group; 66%, 63% and 61%, respectively, thought a poor person was more likely to be found guilty. A higher proportion of the younger age group viewed an Irish person as more likely to be found guilty (29%, 22% and 20% respectively).

A review of the data by socio-economic group suggests few differences in the levels of scepticism. Of the professional/managerial group, 46% thought the black defendant would be more likely to be found guilty compared with 40% of junior non-manual, 43% of skilled manual and 44% of semi/unskilled manual. The views expressed about the likelihood of a poor defendant being found guilty were also similar, with 65% of the professional group thinking the poor person would be found guilty and 60%, 70% and 63% of the other groups, respectively.

Young people's views on ways of preventing crime

Successive crime surveys have suggested that up to three-quarters of crime goes unreported by the victims. A review of the clear-up rates for those offences which are reported reveals that although around 75% of some crimes are resolved (offences of violence, for example), perpetrators of other crimes are very likely to go un-apprehended. Indeed, those crimes which are least likely to be reported (such as criminal damage and theft from vehicles) are also least likely to be cleared up (in 1993 in England and Wales, the clear-up rates for these two crimes were 16% and 13% respectively). Doubtless, these two phenomena are related. The clear-up rate for all notifiable offences was 25% in England and Wales in 1993. The picture is slightly better in Scotland (34%) and Northern Ireland (36%) (HMSO, 1995b: 159)

It is an inescapable fact that the majority of resources devoted to the criminal justice system end up being spent on a very small proportion of the crime actually committed. This may lead one to conclude that a more cost-effective approach to crime would be one that emphasized crime prevention rather than detection and prosecution. Unfortunately, however difficult it may be to catch criminals, it is infinitely harder to develop strategies to prevent them from becoming criminals in the first place. The debate about the most effective ways of preventing crime raises fundamental questions about the nature of human behaviour and development. Do people turn to criminal behaviour (or not as the case may be) because of factors in their family background, the kind of discipline they experience at home or school, or is such behaviour the result of inadequate deterrence? Can we best prevent crime by increasing the resources of the criminal justice system to ensure that more offenders get caught and are locked up, or is it necessary to intervene at the social level to address the root causes of crime? Are would-be offenders stimulated to commit crime by exposure to crime and violence in the media? Studies of the factors correlated with criminal behaviour seldom produce easy answers, though a number of important longitudinal studies (Wadsworth, 1979; Kolvin *et al.*, 1990) have provided a degree of illumination. One of the most important British studies, the Cambridge Institute of Criminology cohort study, has for over 30 years produced data on possible causes and correlations of offending behaviour. In 1982, West identified five key factors that were associated with a member of the study cohort becoming an offender: coming from a low-income family, coming from a large family, having parents considered to be poor at child-rearing, having below average intelligence and having a parent with a criminal record. Of the cohort members who had three or more of these characteristics, almost half became 'delinquent' compared with a fifth of the sample as a whole (West, 1982). More recently, Utting *et al.* (1993) have reviewed the relationship between crime and the family. Farrington (the director of the Cambridge cohort study since 1982) has called for further research to address the perplexing questions about the links between child-rearing and delinquency (Farrington, 1994: 14).

Although many people share a 'common-sense' view that parenting and other social factors such as poverty, low educational attainment and peer group influences affect the likelihood of someone becoming an offender, the challenge for crime prevention policy-makers is to translate such knowledge into clearly defined objectives. It is perhaps not surprising that policies addressing crime prevention tend to be geared towards more easily measurable and shorter-term goals. Bringing about changes in the social environment may be more effective in the long run, but under pressure to respond to crime, it is politically more expedient to point to increased spending on the police and prisons.

If policy-makers are uncertain as to the best ways of preventing crime, it is not surprising that the general public has mixed views. Surveys of adults indicate that most people believe that crime has social causes, but also want more spending on traditional approaches to criminal justice, such as more visible policing and 'stiffer sentences'.

As far as young people are concerned, the Furnham and Gunter survey found that stronger policing was regarded as the best way of preventing crime, with 61% of young people believing this. Females were more likely to hold this opinion (67% of females compared with 57% of males). Asked about the causes of crime, 37% agreed with the statement that 'Crime is caused by people without morals or standards'; 44% agreed with the statement 'Most criminals will never be able to live right no matter how much we do for them'. However, 48% agreed with the statement 'Crime is more often the fault of society than the criminal'(Farnham and Gunter, 1989: 53–4) This latter view is reflected in the responses of young people in the YPSA survey. Just as young people see poverty as a determinant of justice, they also perceive it as an important factor which contributes to crime. Asked about a range of approaches which could be used to prevent crime, 77% expressed the view that reducing poverty would either be 'very effective' or 'quite effective' in reducing crime.

Views on crime prevention

Here are some possible ways of helping to prevent crime in Britain. How effective do you think each one is?

	Very effective	Quite effective	Not very effective	Not at all effective
	%	%	%	%
Less violence on television	11	40	39	9
Religion	6	26	47	19
More prison	17	42	30	8
Less prison	2	16	49	28
Family discipline	24	54	15	4
School discipline	22	56	19	2
Less poverty	28	49	14	4

School and family discipline are also viewed as important, with 78% of young people thinking that more discipline in schools and 78% thinking that more discipline by families would help to reduce crime. Young people view prison as fairly effective, with 59% believing that sending more people to prison would be effective in preventing crime, compared with 18% who think that sending fewer people to prison would be effective. Taking religion more seriously is not regarded as an effective means of crime prevention: 66% thought that this would be not very or not at all effective compared with 32% who thought it would be very or quite effective. There are mixed views about the effects of violence and crime on television, with 51% thinking that reducing this would be very or quite effective and 48% thinking it would be not very or not at all effective.

Gender, age and socio-economic differences in views on crime prevention

- Young women and girls were slightly more inclined to believe that reducing crime and violence on television would be effective: 60% of females thought reducing crime on television would be very or quite effective compared with 44% of boys and young men.
- There was little difference between males and females in their views on the effectiveness of religion being taken more seriously: 34% of males and 32% of females thought this would be very or quite effective.
- Similar views were held by males and females on the effectiveness of prison: 60% of males and 59% of females thought that sending more people to prison would be very or quite effective; 17% of males and 21% of females thought sending fewer people to prison would be very or quite effective.
- Firm discipline in the family and at school were regarded as equally important by males and females: 79% of males and 77% of females thought family discipline would be very or quite effective; 80% of males and 77% of females thought school discipline would be very or quite effective.
- Seventy-nine per cent of males and 75% of females thought reducing poverty would be very or quite effective.
- The younger age group was slightly more inclined to think that reducing crime on television would be very or quite effective, with 54% of 12–15's, 48% of 16–17's and 43% of 18–19's thinking this.
- Older young people were more inclined to think that family discipline is important with 84% of 18–19's thinking that this would be very or quite effective compared with 80% of 16–17's and 76% of 12–15's.
- The younger age group were slightly less inclined to think that reducing poverty would be effective with 21% of 12–15's thinking this would be not very or not at all effective compared with 14% of 16–17's and 14% of 18–19's.

- There were few socio-economic group differences although the approach of sending more people to prison found less favour in the higher groups (13% of the professional group thought this would be very effective, rising to 21% of semi/unskilled manual).

Religious faith and political allegiance and beliefs on crime prevention

The table below shows the percentage of believers and non-believers who thought that particular crime prevention measures would be very or quite effective.

Religious faith and views on crime prevention

	Don't believe in God	**Believe in God now, did not before**	**Have always believed in God**
	%	%	%
Less crime on television	43	56	54
Religion	16	39	43
More prison	56	62	58
Less prison	22	20	18
Family discipline	76	79	81
School discipline	77	78	80
Less poverty	79	76	78

Predictably, over twice as many believers as non-believers thought that taking religion more seriously would be effective against crime. Believers were also slightly more inclined to view family discipline and reducing crime on television as more effective.

The table on the next page shows the percentage of young people who thought that particular crime prevention measures would be very or quite effective by party political allegiance.

It is perhaps not surprising that young Conservative supporters would be slightly more in favour of prison and discipline in the family and at school. What is a little more surprising is the higher percentage of Labour supporters who think that taking religion more seriously would be effective against crime and the similar numbers of Conservatives and Liberal Democrats who think that reducing poverty would be very or quite effective.

Party political allegiance and views on crime prevention

	Conservative	Labour	Liberal Democrats
	%	%	%
Less violence on television	46	52	55
Religion	26	40	27
More prison	65	58	55
Less prison	11	21	20
Family discipline	85	77	79
School discipline	83	79	79
Less poverty	81	77	80

Young people's views on dealing with young offenders

The past few years has seen an explosion of political and media attention on the issue of young offenders. Barely has one outcry over young rioters died down than another has arisen over 'joy-riders' or 'bail-bandits'. Such concerns are greeted with despair by many of those working with young people, viewed as a new 'moral panic'. As one commentator has pointed out, "The press would have us believe society is on the brink of collapse." (Pitts, 1995)

Nevertheless, however disproportionate the public and political concern about youth crime, it is impossible to dismiss it as a minor problem. A study carried out by Coopers and Lybrand (1994), on behalf of the Princes Trust, estimated that offences committed by young people aged 10 to 21 years account for approximately 45% of crimes resulting in a conviction or formal caution. The same study gave an estimated total economic and financial cost of crime attributable to young people as approximately £7 billion per annum (Appendix C11).

Despite these figures, criminal statistics reveal a sharp decline in the number of recorded offences attributable to young people in the decade from 1981 to 1991. NACRO (1992) cites a fall of 37% from 175 000 indictable offences in 1981 to 110 900 in 1991. Even taking account of the number of unrecorded offences, demographic changes and the growth of strategies to divert young people from prosecution, there is little evidence that youth crime has actually increased. The criminal career of most young offenders is quite short and the majority of crimes committed are relatively minor property offences. That most young people grow out of crime has been the basis of much thinking in juvenile justice over the past 15 years. Although a high proportion of young people (in this case, young men — juvenile offending still being a predominantly male pursuit) will offend at some point during their adolescence, the vast majority will stop offending by the time they reach their early twenties. The most rational approach, therefore, is to keep them out of the criminal justice system as far as possible. Policies of diversion both from court and from custody have had considerable support since the early 1980s, greatly influenced by the work of 'liberal justice' writers such as Morris *et al.* (1980), Morris and Giller (1987) and Rutherford (1986). Advocates of such policies point to evidence of their success. Of first-time offenders, 75% are cautioned (though there are regional variations in cautioning rates) and most do not re-offend. Of those young people who are prosecuted and found guilty in court, the majority are diverted from custody. The use of custody for young offenders fell from a peak in 1981 when 7900 young people received custodial sentences to just 1800 in 1991 (NACRO, 1992). The emphasis has been on the use of a range of community sentences and even in the 'get tough' era there has been some acknowledgment that for the majority of young offenders, custody is not only inappropriate, it is also ineffective. NACRO (1993) has calculated that over three-quarters of young people sentenced to custody re-offend. At the same time, as Bottoms (1990) has shown, community sentences have achieved a good degree of credibility as effective alternatives to custody. Recently, a study by McGuire (1995) has suggested that retraining rather than imprisonment may hold the key to reducing re-offending.

Many of the lessons learned during the previous decade were enshrined in the 1991 Criminal Justice Act. This was widely welcomed as providing a rational framework for responding to youth crime, with its emphasis on community sentencing, the abolition of custody for young people under 15 years and strict criteria for its use with older young people. The euphoria was short-lived. Soon the concern centred on the 'persistent young offender' who was portrayed as responsible for an inordinate amount of crime and was cocking a snook at the justice system. These concerns became enmeshed with worries about very serious young offenders. Even though the crimes committed by persistent offenders are not necessarily serious, and very serious crimes committed by young people are thankfully rare, the two phenomena seemed to merge as a single public anxiety about the state of youth. Only five months after the implementation of the 1991 Act, the Home Secretary was announcing the introduction of a secure training order to be aimed at that comparatively small group of very persistent juvenile offenders whose repeated offending makes them a menace to the community.

Defining the persistent young offender is not necessarily a simple task. Predicting which offenders will become persistent is even more problematic. Hagell and Newburn (1994) considered three possible definitions of persistence in their study of 531 young offenders: a definition based on frequency of all offences; a definition based on frequency of offending over a three-month period; a definition based on the criteria for the secure training order (all children aged 12–14 who commit three or more imprisonable offences and whose current offence is deemed serious enough to warrant such an order). All the young people in their sample were re-offenders but fewer than a quarter had been arrested more than five times in the previous year. Applying each of the definitions produced a slightly different group of young people each time. Of the 25 young people who met the third definition, only eight met either of the two other definitions. Interviews with a sample of re-offenders provided a picture of young people with chaotic lives, characterized by disrupted school and family history and significant levels of drug and alcohol misuse. Hagell and Newburn, however, found little to distinguish those 'persistent young offenders' who fitted one or more of the definitions from the sample of re-offenders as a whole. The difficulty in predicting which young person is likely to go on to become a persistent offender has implications for deciding how a first-time offender should be dealt with — by diversion or deterrence.

So, what is believed to be the best way of dealing with a young person who commits crime? Should he be kept out of the justice system in the expectation that he will grow out of his offending in due course? Should he be deterred from further offending by punishment in the community, or by the 'short, sharp shock' of custody?

The *1994 British Social Attitudes Survey* suggests that the trend among adults is towards a more punitive approach to offenders. In 1993, 85% of respondents agreed with the statement, 'People who break the law should be given stiffer sentences', an increase from 78% in 1989 and 72% in 1986 (Ahrendt and Young 1994: 85).

The young people in the YPSA survey seem rather less punitive in their outlook. They seem to be particularly supportive of the idea of community service for first-time young offenders. There is widespread acceptance of the view that young people should not be sent to adult prisons.

Young people were asked to give their views on how someone under 16 who had committed a burglary for the first time should be dealt with and their responses are shown in the table on the following page.

A substantial number of young people felt that a special institution for young offenders would be the best punishment for the first-time burglar. In fact, the majority of first offenders are cautioned (depending on the seriousness of the offence and subject to some regional variations) which would meet with the approval of just over a quarter of the sample. Almost half would not actually lock up a first-time burglar but would want them to pay for their crime by community service. The picture emerges of young people who are not very punitive in their outlook but neither are they 'soft' on crime.

Views on dealing with a first-time, under-sixteen burglar

How much are you in favour or against:

	Strongly in favour	In favour	Neither for nor against	Against	Strongly Against
	%	%	%	%	%
Warning	15	38	16	25	5
Community Service	19	62	9	8	1
Institution	9	26	19	37	8
Prison	4	6	8	43	38

What is the best way of dealing with such a young person?

	%
Give them a strong warning but leave them to their parents to sort out	27
Make them spend a certain amount of time helping people in the community	50
Send them to a special institution for young offenders	21
Send them to an ordinary prison for adult criminals	2

Gender, age and socio-economic differences in views of dealing with young offenders

The data analysed by gender suggest that although community service is viewed slightly more favourably by females, slightly more males are inclined to favour a strong warning for the first-time burglar.

Gender and views on the best way of dealing with a first-time, under-sixteen burglar

	Males	Females
	%	%
Strong warning	31	24
Community service	47	53
Special institution	20	21
Adult prison	3	1

Viewing the data by age (see the table on the next page), the favourable view of community service is shared across all three age bands but is particularly marked in the 16–17 age group (62% favouring this option) with a higher proportion of the 12–15's being in favour of a strong warning (30%).

Age and views on the best way of dealing with a first-time, under-sixteen burglar

	Age group		
	12–15	**16–17**	**18–19**
	%	%	%
Strong warning	31	19	23
Community service	45	62	48
Special institution	22	17	23
Adult prison	2	1	4

There are few differences between socio-economic groups, as shown in the table below.

Socio-economic group and views on the best way of dealing with a first-time, under-sixteen burglar

	Group			
	1	**3**	**4**	**5**
	%	%	%	%
Strong warning	24	24	34	25
Community service	54	52	44	47
Special institution	21	21	17	23
Adult prison	1	2	4	2

Group 1 (professional/managerial) and Group 2 (intermediate non-manual) were combined into Group 1 for the purposes of analysis as the numbers in 2 were very small. Group 3 (junior non-manual); Group 4 (skilled manual); and Group 5 (semi-skilled and unskilled manual) are also shown.

Faith and political allegiance and views on dealing with young offenders

An analysis by faith suggests a slightly more punitive outlook on the part of non-believers, with slightly fewer non-believers supporting the option of a warning (25% compared with 28% of those who believe now but did not before and 29% of those who have always believed) and slightly more supporting an institution (21% compared with 14% and 20%, respectively).

A higher percentage of Labour supporters favour a strong warning for the first-time offender (29% compared with 23% of Liberal Democrats and

18% of Conservatives), though 3% of Labour supporters would favour sending him to an adult prison (none of the Conservative or Liberal Democrats identifiers chose this as the best way of dealing with the first-time offender). Otherwise, there are relatively few differences by political allegiance.

Young people's views on the death penalty

Among adults, the overall support for the death penalty has remained at around 65% (Ahrendt and Young, 1994).

Furnham and Gunter (1989) found that the young people in their survey were largely in favour of the death penalty: 66% endorsed capital punishment for murderers.

The young people in the YPSA survey expressed similar views on capital punishment: 34% of young people thought that British courts should definitely be able to sentence murderers to death; 30% thought they should probably be able to; 17% thought they definitely should not be able to use the death sentence.

Gender, age and socio-economic differences in views on the death penalty

The *British Social Attitudes Survey* among adults consistently shows more females in favour of the death penalty than males. These findings were echoed in the Furnham and Gunter (1989) study which found 70% of females and 65% of males in favour. Interestingly, the YPSA survey rather bucks this trend (see table below), with similar percentages of males and females believing that courts should definitely or probably be able to sentence murderers to death, but rather more females than males being definitely against.

Gender and views on whether British courts should be able to sentence murderers to death

	Male	**Female**
	%	%
Definitely	35	33
Probably	30	30
Probably not	18	14
Definitely not	14	21

Age appears to be a more significant variable than gender in this survey, with the table below showing a rise in the number of young people in favour of the death penalty with age.

Age and views on whether British courts should be able to sentence murderers to death

	Age group		
	12–15	**16–17**	**18–19**
	%	%	%
Definitely	30	34	52
Probably	31	29	26
Probably not	17	16	13
Definitely not	19	18	9

There are some interesting differences between socio-economic groups in views on the death penalty. Young people in the professional group are less in favour of it than those in other groups with a very marked difference between group 1 and group 5, shown in the table.

% in socio-economic group and views on whether British courts should be able to sentence murderers to death

	Group			
	1	**3**	**4**	**5**
Definitely	28	28	37	49
Probably	30	39	31	21
Probably not	18	13	18	13
Definitely not	23	19	11	10

Group 1 (professional/managerial) and Group 2 (intermediate non-manual) were combined into Group 1 for the purposes of analysis as the numbers in 2 were very small. Group 3 (junior non-manual); Group 4 (skilled manual); and Group 5 (semi-skilled and unskilled manual) are also shown.

Political allegiance and views on the death penalty

Slightly more Labour supporters (39%) expressed the view that courts should definitely have the power to use the death sentence compared with

Conservative (31%) and Liberal Democrats (34%). However, twice as many Liberal Democrat supporters (30%) were totally opposed to this compared with the other two parties (Conservative, 16%; Labour, 14%).

Conclusion

Crime is seen as an important issue by young people but not necessarily of paramount importance. A survey of young adults (aged between 18 and 34) carried out by MORI (1990) asked the question: 'What do you see as important issues facing Britain over the next 10 years or so?' Crime was mentioned by 13% of young adults and ranked equal eighth in the list of 19 most commonly cited issues. It shared this ranking with AIDS and was above housing (10%), education (10%) and nuclear weapons (7%) but below the health service (14%) and way below the top-ranked issue of the environment (46%) (MORI, 1990: 1–2).

These findings are reassuring in an era when any exposure to the media can lead one to feel that crime has overwhelmed all other issues as a focus of concern.

Nevertheless, this survey suggests that crime has touched on the lives of the great majority of young people in Britain today. Even children as young as 12 are more likely than not to have experienced crime as a victim. This personal exposure to crime as well as the experience of it through the media has no doubt influenced young people's worries about becoming a victim. Yet there is little evidence that such worries are out of proportion. Many young people still feel comparatively safe in their area and a picture emerges of young people taking sensible precautions against crime but still getting on with their lives without allowing fear to daunt them unduly.

Young people show a considerable awareness of inequalities and discrimination on the grounds of race and poverty. Significant numbers of young people express doubts about the ability of courts to act fairly and even-handedly towards black and poor defendants. Given the number of well-publicized miscarriages of justice over the past few years, this is perhaps not surprising. What may be more surprising in view of the wide publicity concerning cases of the Guildford Four and the Birmingham Six, is that there is rather less perceived discrimination against Irish people.

In their views on the ways of preventing crime, young people seem largely of the opinion that it is important to address the causes of crime. Poverty is seen as one of the main causes of crime, with over three-quarters of young people thinking that the reduction of poverty would be an effective means of crime prevention. The role of discipline in the family and in schools is regarded as equally important. Prison is seen as an important deterrent, with almost 60% of young people thinking that sending more people to prison would be very or quite effective against crime. However, fewer young people (just over half) are convinced of the association between crime and violence on television and crime that occurs in real life.

When asked about the best way of dealing with a juvenile burglar after their first offence, most young people were neither harsh nor 'soft' in their views. Almost half favoured community service and just over a quarter felt a strong warning would suffice. In general, young people were opposed to locking up a first-time offender and were very clear that it was not appropriate to use an adult prison for such a purpose: over 80% of young people were opposed to this. Young people were generally in favour of capital punishment as an option for sentencing in murder cases: 64% were either definitely or probably in favour, a similar percentage to adults.

Taken overall, the views expressed by young people about the issue of crime are not radically different from those of adults. Young people are aware of crime, are to some extent fearful of it, and take sensible precautions to avoid it but there is no evidence that such concerns dominate the lives of young people. On the other hand, young people are not oblivious to the effects of crime and are very often victims of it. This is a factor frequently overlooked in our preoccupation with young people as offenders.

Perhaps the most striking aspect of the views expressed by young people is the level of disillusionment with the justice system in terms of its ability to deal fairly with all defendants regardless of race and income. Young people express balanced views on ways of preventing crime and dealing with a young offender. The findings of the survey suggest that young people are aware both of the underlying social factors which can lead to crime and of the need to deter the individual offender. There is strong support for the concept of the offender being made to pay for his crime in the form of community service rather than by being locked up. This may provide some solace as we prepare for the advent of boot camps.

References

Ahrendt, D. and Young, K. (1994), 'Authoritarianism updated', in Jowell, R., Curtice, J., Brook, L. and Ahrendt, D. (eds), *British Social Attitudes: the 11th report*, Aldershot: Dartmouth.

Bottoms, A. (1990), *Intermediate Treatment and Juvenile Justice: Key findings and implications from a national survey of intermediate treatment policy and practice*, London: HMSO.

Brown, I. (1992), *The Criminal Justice System: Schoolchildren speak out*, West Yorkshire Probation Committee.

Central Statistical Office (1995) *Social Trends Management*, London: HMSO.
Cohen, S. (1980), *Folk Devils and Moral Panics*, London: McGibbon & Kee/Paladin.
Coopers and Lybrand (1994), *Preventative Strategies for Young People in Trouble*, London: ITV Telethon and The Prince's Trust.
Coote, A. (ed.) (1994), *Families, Children and Crime*, London: Institute for Public Policy Research.
Downes, D. and Rock, P. (1988), *Understanding Deviance: Guide to the Sociology of Crime and Rule-Breaking*, Buckingham: Open University Press.
Farrington, D. (1994), *The Influence of the Family on Delinquent Development: proceedings of a conference on Crime and the Family*, London: Family Policy Studies Centre.
Fitzgerald, M. (1993), *Ethnic Minorities and the Criminal Justice System: Evidence to the Royal Commission on Criminal Justice*, London: HMSO.
Furnham, A. and Gunter, B. (1989), *The Anatomy of Adolescence: Young People's Social Attitudes in Britain*, London: Routledge.
Hagell, A. and Newburn, T. (1994), *Persistent Young Offenders*, London: Policy Studies Institute.
Hartless, J.M., Ditton, J., Nair, G. and Phillips, S. (1995), 'More Sinned Against Than Sinning: A study of young teenagers' experience of crime', *British Journal of Criminology*, **35**, 1: 114–33.
HMSO (1992), *Criminal Statistics for England and Wales*, London: HMSO.
HMSO (1993), *The 1992 British Crime Survey*, London: HMSO.
HMSO (1995), *Regional Trends*, London: HMSO.
Hudson, B. (1987), *Justice Through Punishment*, London: Macmillan.
Kolvin, I., Miller, F.J.W., Scott, D.M., Gatzanis, S.R.M. and Fleeting, M. (1990), *Continuities of Deprivation?*, Aldershot: Avebury.
Leeds Mercury (1869), February.
McGuire, J. (ed.) (1995), *What Works — Reducing Offending*, Chichester: Wiley.
MORI (1990), *Young Britain: a survey of 18–34 year olds*, A research study conducted for the Reader's Digest, London: MORI.
Morris, A. and Giller, H. (1987), *Understanding Juvenile Justice*, London: Croom Helm.
Morris, A., Giller, H., Szwed, E. and Geach, H. (1980), *Justice for Children*, London: Macmillan.
Muncie, J. (1984), *The Trouble with Kids Today*, London: Hutchinson.
NACRO (1991), *The Criminal Justice Act 1991: implications for juvenile and young adult offenders*, London: NACRO.
NACRO (1992), *Some Facts About Juvenile Crime*, London: NACRO.
NACRO (1993), *Juvenile Crime: Some current issues*, London: NACRO.
Pearson, G. (1983), *Hooligan: A history of respectable fears*, London: Macmillan.
Pitts, J. (1995), 'Scare in the Community: Part 1: youth crime', *Community Care* 4–10 May: i–viii.
Rutherford, A. (1986), *Growing out of Crime*, Harmondsworth: Penguin.
Rutter, M. and Giller, H. (1983), *Juvenile Delinquency — Trends and Perspectives*, Harmondsworth: Penguin.
Tarling, R. (1993), *Analysing Offending: Data, models and interpretations*, London: HMSO.
Utting, D., Bright, J. and Henricson, C. (1993), *Crime and the Family*, London: Family Policy Studies Centre.
Wadsworth, M. (1979), *Roots of Delinquency*, London: Martin Robertson.
West, D. (1982), *Delinquency: Its roots, careers and prospects*, London: Heinemann.

5 Young people: stakeholders in the educational system

MIKE HUGHES AND EVA LLOYD

Most young people currently in the educational system in England and Wales will have experienced considerable change and sometimes disruption within the last few years. The curriculum changes associated with the introduction of the National Curriculum, the fact that Standard Assessment Tests were boycotted in a sizeable number of schools, the introduction of new official guidance on sex and religious education, and schools' subsequent development of policies in these areas, as well as the move towards Grant Maintained status, influencing both pupil intake and educational programmes, are all likely to have had a direct effect on pupils' everyday experiences at school.

The 1993 *British Social Attitudes* (BSA) *Survey* report investigated the reaction of adults, in particular parents, to recent educational upheavals (Halsey and Lievesley, 1994) and concluded that many of their findings were encouraging for the educational system, with a reasonable level of confidence in the academic standards being attained by schools. There did not appear to be public demand for radical reform.

However, although the perspectives of parents, teachers and policy-makers on educational strategies and practices continue to receive sustained publicity, the views of young people themselves are rarely heard. The *Young People's Social Attitudes* (YPSA) *Survey* contributes to a new trend in line with the provision of Article 12 of the UN Convention on the Rights of the Child. This deals with the young person's right to express an opinion and for due consideration to be given to such opinions.

The survey of young people's attitudes towards some key aspects of education highlights the views of an important section of its 'consumers'. It provides the opportunity to compare young people's attitudes with those of adults in their own as well as in other households on a range of educational questions which have also been asked of adults in previous surveys. These cover standards of attainment and how they are appraised, parental say in what is taught in schools, and disciplinary policies. In addition, young people only were asked specific questions pertinent to their lives at school, on sex education, drug use in school and dealing with bullying.

The importance of education in the eyes of young people was demonstrated in the survey: the intrinsic value of education, how it should be structured and delivered, and its moral content were all taken very seriously. Not only was personal and social development considered (by addressing sex education) but the codes of conduct surrounding the school setting were examined, and the social norms required of young people, their parents and teachers, were all highlighted.

Young people's attitudes to three aspects of education were examined within the survey: aspects of curriculum, standards of attainment and how they are appraised, and aspects of behaviour.

In relation to each of these three matters, variations according to certain basic variables were considered: gender, age, racial origin, and to a lesser extent religious belief, social class and household composition. The sample selected for the YPSA survey contained very few respondents from the Asian (32) and black (6) communities. It is, therefore, not possible to draw strong conclusions from the responses when differentiated for ethnic origin. Consequently, none of the analysis of racial differentiation is represented in tabular form, but is included in the commentary on the tables.

Curriculum

To what extent should aspects of the curriculum be determined by parents and children? Strong views on this were held by the respondents, and with hindsight one would have wished for a view to be given in addition on the respective weight that should be given to education professionals in this matter. Young people's views on parental determination of curriculum are summarized in the table below.

Parental influence on the curriculum: young people's views

How much say should parents have in what is taught in school?

	%
All of the say	6
Quite a bit of the say	39
Some of the say	47
Not very much say	5
No say at all	2
Don't know	<1

Male and female responses were very closely aligned. It is clear that virtually every young person felt that parents should have an input into curriculum determination. Views varied slightly on the extent, but clearly they have a role in the eyes of young people.

There were slight variations between black, Asian and white respondents, but given the low numbers of ethnic minority respondents, it is unsafe to draw strong conclusions from these variations; nor is there much fluctuation in pattern when age differentiation is considered. Parental say is marginally more important for those young people who said that they had always believed in God. Those young people with the strongest predisposition towards parental say were in the highest socio-economic group.

How far do the moderate views expressed here coincide with adult attitudes? The question 'How much say should parents have in what is taught in school?' was put to the adult sample and the responses were very similar indeed to those of the young people. The congruence is even more marked when the views of the young people are set alongside those of adults from the same households as YPSA respondents.

Parental influence on the curriculum: adult and young people's views compared

How much say should parents have in what is taught in school?

	Adults[1]	**Parents**[2]	**Young people**
	%	%	%
All of the say	8	7	6
Quite a bit/some of the say	80	88	86
Not very much say	9	5	5
No say at all	3	<1	2

[1] All adults interviewed for the 1994 BSA survey who were asked this question.
[2] Those adults/parents asked this question in the 1994 BSA survey in households where a young person was interviewed for YPSA.

These similarities are explored in the following table. Although these adults were the young person's parent in the majority of cases, care must be taken not to make the automatic assumption that the attitude expressed is that of 'the parents'.

It would have been interesting to know current adult attitudes to children having a say in what is taught in schools to see whether messages such as those from the UN Convention and from the Children Act 1989 are percolating through to the population in an area where traditionally children and young people's views have been virtually ignored (UN Committee, 1995: 6). However, adult BSA respondents were not asked about how much say children should have in the school curriculum.

Children, too, should have a say in what is taught in school: this was the majority view, in the YPSA survey, although this majority was not quite as overwhelming as that which said that parents should have a say.

The say of parents and children in what is taught in school: views of young people

	Yes[1]	No[2]
	%	%
Should parents have a say?	92	7
Should children have a say?	74	24

[1] This includes responses of young people who selected the options 'all of the say', 'quite a bit of the say' or 'some of the say'.
[2] This includes responses of young people who selected the options 'not very much say' or 'no say at all'.

The one area of the curriculum where parental input has been actively sought has been that of sex education and it was included in the 1994 survey, but only young people themselves were quizzed about it. This area merits separate discussion, and is dealt with below.

The 1993 BSA survey confirmed that parents want to share responsibility with teachers for their children's education, and highlighted some of the means by which parents tried to achieve this (Halsey and Lievesley, 1994: 105). In the case of graduate parents, this meant attendance at parents' evenings and meetings with individual teachers to discuss their secondary school children's progress. For young people, the development of school councils may be one way to present them with increasing opportunities to have a say in their school lives. In the area of more general educational strategies at secondary level, similar discrepancies become apparent between parental and pupil perspectives and the views of the relevant authorities evident from prevailing practice. We also need to ensure, when referring to parental participation, that we are clear whether we are dealing with either curriculum, or consultation process. Do we merely want to ensure that parents are seen to be given the opportunity to speak, or are there also interests which say that parents should be more significant determinants? This is not simply a matter of degree.

Is there something of a myth about how much say respective interests can have? Would teachers feel that they have a say? Would headteachers?

A different, but related, question was considered, namely the age at which curriculum choices are made. About one-third of the young respondents agreed that pupils were too young when they had to decide which subjects to specialize in. There was little gender differentiation in responses, and quite a strong message of dissatisfaction with being forced into premature choices. Conversely, almost two-thirds of the respondents either 'strongly disagreed' or 'disagreed' with the statement that the present law allows pupils to leave school when they are too young. The duration of the school experience was approved, but the balance of content challenged.

Adults were asked these same questions as part of the 1987 and 1990 surveys (Halsey, 1991: 54) but not in 1994. On those earlier occasions, two-thirds of adults felt that secondary pupils are too young when obliged to decide which subjects to specialize in, whereas only about a third of the 1994 young people's cohort feel that way, and another third actually disagreed. In the same years, only about a quarter of the adult sample thought the school-leaving age was too low, compared with about one-fifth of the young people interviewed in 1994. So on this subject, earlier samples of adult respondents and today's young people appear to share similar views.

It is not so long since the school-leaving age was raised from 15 to 16. It appears to have become very strongly accepted by the community. Indeed, there are strong signs of many more young people staying on beyond the compulsory school age. For example, in one metropolitan borough, 75% of 16-year-olds stay on at least a further year. Some of this represents the enhanced value placed on education, although we must recognize that for many others it represents the only viable alternative to doing nothing.

Sex education

The 1993 Education Act made sex education a compulsory subject in secondary schools while giving parents the right to withdraw their children. Since the 1986 Education (No 2) Act, the governors of county and controlled primary and secondary schools have already had a duty to formulate a policy on sex education, although they could decide not to include sex education in the curriculum. Consultation with and involvement of parents were seen as central aims in the changes effected by this Act, and it was found that the majority of parents were keen for schools to teach this subject (Allen, 1987).

By 1991, a survey of education authorities in England and Wales (Thomson and Scott, 1992) had found that of the two-thirds of primary schools with a policy in place at that time, only 5% had decided against including sex education in the curriculum. These facts throw an interesting light on the attitudes expressed by the young people in this survey.

Compulsory sex education in schools for children under 11 was not considered desirable by most young people — two-thirds felt that it should be left to parental choice. This was particularly a view expressed by those in the youngest age band of the respondents (12–15-year-olds). Children and young people from families with two parents tended to place slightly greater emphasis on parental choice in this matter (63%) than young people with one parent in the household (59%). Sex education for 12–16-year-olds presented a slightly different profile. These data are summarized in the table below.

Views on sex education for children

	%
All children aged 11 and under should have sex education at school	37
All children aged 12–16 years should have sex education at school	53
Parents should be allowed to choose	9

Evidently the vast majority of those who did not respond positively to under-eleven's receiving sex education believed that secondary school children should receive it. There were some fluctuations — for example, children from two-parent households were slightly more likely (54%) to believe that all children of secondary age should receive sex education at school compared with those from single-parent families (50%).

In contrast, a 1994 telephone survey of a representative sample of 13–15-year-olds commissioned by the Health Education Authority (HEA) showed half of them to be in favour of providing sex education to children aged 11 and under, with girls more likely to think this than boys (Family Planning Association, 1994). Just as in the YPSA survey, the HEA cohort largely reject the parental right to withdraw their children from this programme within the secondary curriculum, but virtually the whole HEA cohort believes that all young people should receive such education at school.

It is perhaps disappointing to find that no more than half of the YPSA survey respondents believed that all secondary school pupils should receive sex education in school in the light of what is currently known about the likely long-term effects of such an intervention. The British national survey of sexual attitudes and lifestyles (Johnson *et al.*, 1994) confirmed the possibility of a positive and protective association between school sex education and sexual behaviour. This, the researchers claim, was in line with a review of 35 studies carried out by the WHO Global Programme on AIDS which found no evidence that sex education leads to earlier or increased sexual activity in young people (Wellings *et al.*, 1995: 417).

Speculating about the factors underlying the opinions expressed in the table above, one might wonder if an important lesson for health educators may be concealed behind these attitudes. Is it the kind of sex education they receive, rather than sex education *per se* which young people reject by means of this response? Should education of this kind be based on what young people themselves say they want and need in terms of sexual health information and resources? And should it be based on sound evidence of their effectiveness in terms of behaviour rather than knowledge or attitudes alone? Suggestions to this effect were made in a recent methodological review of sexual health education interventions with young people (Oakley *et al.*, 1995). Revisiting these issues in future surveys could prove informative.

Standards in education

Educational achievement is highly prized by young people. They said unequivocally that this was one of the most valuable factors for doing well in life, as shown in the table on the following page.

Boys (29%) placed slightly greater emphasis than girls (22%) on the essential role of education for future success, but the strongest message is that all young people value the contribution made by education to their future. Again, we would draw attention to the point made above about the reason for staying on at school being a balance between anything else being available and a recognition about the value of education for the future.

The survey addressed the respective emphasis given to examinations and class work (see the second table on the following page). Opinion was divided on the value of formal examinations as a means of judging ability. However, if 'neutral' responses are excluded, the balance of opinion is in favour of valuing exams as a means of judging ability. Girls were slightly less confident about the value of exams than boys.

Importance of education in doing well in life

Now some questions about doing well in life. How important is having a good education yourself?

	Male	Female
	%	%
Essential	29	22
Very important	54	54
Fairly important	15	23
Not very important	2	<1
Not at all important	0	1

Views on the value of exams

How much do you agree or disagree with the statement about secondary schooling: 'Formal exams are the best way of judging the ability of pupils?'

	Male	Female
	%	%
Agree strongly	7	6
Agree	40	39
Neither agree/disagree	15	13
Disagree	32	32
Disagree strongly	4	8

This needs to be set alongside the views of young people about the weight that is given to classwork. The responses are not entirely reconcilable. On the one hand, 46% of young people 'agreed strongly' or 'agreed' with the statement that examinations are the best way to judge ability, 63% also 'agreed strongly' or 'agreed' with the statement that 'so much attention is given to exam results in Britain that a pupil's everyday classroom work counts for too little'.

Attitudes of these young people towards the relative weight accorded to exam results and class results in assessing school performance can be set against those of adults. The attitudes of adults towards this topic have been explored three times in the last eight years. It has remained much the same between 1987 and 1993. Around two-thirds agree with the opinion that a pupil's everyday classroom work counts for too little, while the percentage of those who consider that formal exams are the best way of judging the ability of pupils has crept up from 44% to 53% in that period (Halsey and

Lievesley, 1994: 99). On this issue, too, adult and pupil opinions would seem to converge.

There was a slightly greater reluctance on the part of Asian young people (although we should bear in mind the small numbers here) and those from professional families, to place their confidence in examinations. Those who had always held religious beliefs had greater confidence in them.

The finding that value appears to be attached to examinations themselves and the qualifications associated with them, not only by the adults but also by the young people, is echoed in findings from a Policy Studies Institute survey of young people in their final year of compulsory education (Shaw, 1994a, 1994b, 1994c). Amongst a large, though not nationally representative, sample of 16- and 17-year-olds in inner-city areas studied by Shaw, well over two-thirds thought exams were important in securing a job, were not a waste of time and that failing exams would adversely affect people's life chances (Shaw, 1994b: 31). We can only speculate that similar considerations inspired the responses to the questions posed as part of the YPSA survey. We can hope that the convergence in views detected by this survey between adults and young people within the same household contributes to harmony in real life between the educational aspirations of parents for their children and those of the young people themselves.

So, attainment, it is clear, is of great significance to the young person. The same applies to the overall attainment of the school, at least so far as secondary education is concerned. Most respondents emphasized the value of the publication of secondary school results, but they were not so convinced about the merit of reporting on the results of testing junior school children. The two sets of responses are set alongside each other in the following table.

Publication of test results

How useful is it for parents if:

	Very useful %	**Quite useful** %	**Not really useful** %
Secondary schools publish their exam results	30	50	17
Schools for children aged 7–11 published their test results	12	37	48

It could reasonably be argued that young people aged 12 to 19 would take secondary examination results more seriously than they would tests for

7 to 11-year-olds — the secondary examinations are either on their horizon or a recent experience, and they would clearly see these as having a greater impact on their lives. This is further illustrated by the age-differentiated attitude to the publication of secondary examination results in the table below. Although this question was not about the importance of examinations themselves, it is reasonable to infer from views about the importance of publication of results a valuation of the examinations themselves.

Age differences in views on the publication of secondary results

	Very useful	Quite useful	Not really useful
	%	%	%
12–15-year-olds	28	52	15
16–17-year-olds	31	50	19
18–19-year-olds	35	44	20

Respondents had some reservations about the value of publishing examination results. Those in the oldest group were the most decided in their view that publishing was of value, whereas the youngest group offered the most moderate profile.

Much of the publicity given to 'league tables' in education has been directed at parents, so it is useful that the 1994 YPSA survey allows a comparison between their views and those of young people. Young people's attitudes towards the publication of secondary exam results were set next to both those of the adult sample as a whole and those of the sample of adults sharing the households of the young people interviewed. Most adults, whether living with the young people or not, thought that their publication was either 'very useful' or 'quite useful'. Of all adults 20% thought that it was not really useful, and of the 'parents' 23%. There were no great discrepancies here between adult and youthful views.

In the case of test results for children between the ages of 7 and 11, the adults in general were slightly more positive than the adults sharing a household with a young person interviewed, among whom we may assume were a majority of their parents. The views of the young people interviewed for YPSA, on this issue, were more in line with the 'parents' interviewed in the same household as the young people than with the total adult sample interviewed for BSA.

Behaviour

The behaviour of young people in relation to the school system is of particular concern to Barnardo's: first, the organization provides many services that are either schools or short-term alternatives to school. In addition, many more Barnardo's projects also focus on aspects of education, and others are concerned with matters of behaviour and justice.

In relation to policy and research, Barnardo's is concerned with influencing legislation and guidelines on behaviour management in schools. For example, a study was conducted by Barnardo's and Family Service Units into the consequences for family life of excluding children from school. It is from this sound practice, policy and research background that Barnardo's comments on the attitudes that young people have demonstrated to school behaviour (Cohen *et al.*, 1994).

Bullying in school was seen to be a significant, if not overwhelming, issue for young people, and views on its prevalence were influenced by a number of variables. First, the relationship of gender and prevalence of bullying is considered, and this is represented in the table below.

Gender and views on prevalence of bullying

Thinking of your current (most recent) school/6th form college. Would you say that students get (got) bullied by other students …

	Male	**Female**
	%	%
a lot	25	30
a little	55	54
not at all	20	15

More than half of the young people felt that bullying occurs to a small extent, but at the extremes there is some gender distinction: girls were slightly more likely to believe that a lot of bullying takes place, and boys more likely to consider that none occurs at all.

Similar slight variations are evident when the question of views on the prevalence of bullying is considered alongside other variables:

- 12–15-year-old respondents (88%) believe that the phenomenon is more widespread (bullying happens 'a lot' or 'a little') than 18–19-year-old ones (73%).

- Those who do not believe in God (22%) are more likely to believe that no bullying takes place than those who have always believed in God (15%).
- Those with one parent (35%) are more likely to believe that bullying happens 'a lot' than those with two parents (26%).

Does this match the public perception of the extent to which bullying occurs, and the attention that the problem has received from Government? A concerted campaign has been conducted by the Department for Education and Employment to show that bullying is seen to be a problem by authorities, and to alert young people to tell an adult if it happens to them. The YPSA survey results would suggest that the campaign was justified and that the problem exists. It is the perception of more than a quarter of the sample that it exists extensively.

The Elton Report (1989) concluded on the basis of a number of studies that bullying appeared to be widespread in schools. From that same year onwards, the Gulbenkian Foundation funded a number of initiatives around this phenomenon (Whitney and Smith, 1993), including a three-month extension to the Childline service to run a special bullying line and the publication of an annotated bibliography on anti-bullying materials and strategies (Skinner, 1992). At first, research focused on establishing the incidence rather than the prevalence of bullying and asked young people about their experiences of being bullied or being bullies themselves (Smith, 1991; Mellor, 1990; O'Moore and Hillery, 1989).

A study among almost 7000 Sheffield primary and secondary pupils by Whitney and Smith (1993) found that 10% of secondary pupils reported being bullied 'sometimes' or more often in any one term, and 4% 'once a week or more', with bullying decreasing the higher up the school they went. The incidence of bullying was much higher among junior and middle school pupils. This, the authors concluded, amounted to bullying on a disturbing scale, although it was still lower than that reported in some other studies in the UK.

It is difficult to compare the responses on its prevalence among the national YPSA sample with this information on incidence in a non-representative sample, but the data appear to point in the same direction. Both the Department for Education and Employment and the Home Office are now funding intervention projects and their effectiveness is being monitored. On the whole the answer to the problem is thought to lie within schools, as far as the authorities are concerned (Kingman, 1994). It is therefore interesting to look at the views of this sample of young people on how bullying should be dealt with in schools (see table below). More than half the young people felt that persistent bullying should be dealt with by taking the offender out of the school system, temporarily or permanently.

Views on dealing with bullies

What do you think should happen to someone who keeps on bullying other students at school? Should they be ...

	%
... expelled from their school	31
... temporarily suspended from their school	26
... dealt with in some other way, but stay at their school	41

Fifty-seven per cent may seem a high proportion to have recommended exclusion, but equally it is impressive that 41% of young people felt that the problem should be contained within the school. There were some interesting variations within the sample:

- Boys (29%) were more likely to favour temporary suspensions than girls (23%), who were slightly more likely to recommend expulsion (33%) than boys (28%).
- Young people from families with one parent (36%) were more likely to favour expulsion than those from families with two parents (30%); the latter declared more strongly in favour of dealing with bullying within the school system (42%) than one-parent families (35%).

School staff are not perceived to be subjected substantially to the threat of violence. It is interesting to set the perceptions of bullying by other students alongside views about violent threats to teachers. This comparison is presented in the table below.

The threat of violence from students is seen to be far greater towards other students than to teachers. This is borne out by the statistics on violence

Threats to teachers and student bullying

Thinking of your current (most recent) school/6th form college. Would you say ...

	... A lot	**... A little**	**... Not at all**
	%	%	%
... students get (got) bullied by other students	27	54	17
... teachers get (got) threatened by students	11	40	46

in schools, and figures for exclusion for reported violence, including violence amongst primary school children. Exclusions of primary school children for acts of violence towards other pupils have increased markedly in recent years.

However, threatening violence to teachers was seen as a far graver matter, albeit less frequent, if the suggested handling of such incidents is anything to go by. The table below sets out the views of young people on dealing with this type of behaviour which can be compared with young people's views on how bullying of other students should be dealt with.

Views on dealing with someone who threatens a teacher

What do you think should happen to someone who keeps on threatening a teacher at school. Should they be...

	%
... expelled from their school	53
... suspended from their school for some time	24
... dealt with in some other way but stay at their school	20

Again, there were a number of variations in attitudes to dealing with those who threatened teachers:

- Girls were far more likely (61%) than boys (46%) to suggest that such offenders should be expelled.
- Respondents from families with two parents (22%) were slightly more likely than those from one-parent families (18%) to see the resolution of the problem as lying within the school.

Drug usage at school was not seen to be extensive, but it was most distinctly there as an issue. Almost half of the respondents said that it occurred, but 'a little.' Less than a fifth said that their experience was that it happened 'a lot.' Younger people reported the usage as less than older respondents.

The prevalence of drug-taking reported here can be compared with data from two surveys of knowledge and experience of drug misuse. A survey of younger users has been conducted at five-yearly intervals since 1969 (Wright and Pearl, 1995). It reported that in 1994, 65% of pupils between 14 and 15 knew someone who took illicit drugs. This percentage rises with age (Parker and Measham, 1994) and may be as much as 90% in the late teens. However, these surveys did not restrict themselves to asking about drug-taking in the students' own schools, as the YPSA survey did, but looked at their wider environment. This might explain its greater prevalence as reported in these surveys.

Views on the gravity of drug usage may be inferred from the fact that the majority of young people felt that persistent drug usage should be punished by expulsion or at least suspension from school (see table below). It is useful to compare this response alongside the views reported above on bullying of students and threats to teachers and on how the various misdemeanours should be dealt with. This represents a tariff of gravity of behaviour in the minds of the respondents.

Views on dealing with drug users

What do you think should happen to someone who keeps on having drugs in school? Should they be ...

	%
... expelled from their school	55
... suspended from their school for some time	14
... dealt with in some other way, but stay at their school	29

Attitudes to how drug possession in school should be dealt with moderated with age. Another interesting variation lies in the fact that Asian young people were markedly more of the view (50%) that the matter should be dealt with in school. This conclusion needs to be treated with caution, as it is derived from a very small number of Asian respondents (32).

So much for insights into young people's attitudes to actual behaviour and how it should be dealt with. Views were also expressed on the extent to which they and their parents should have any say in what punishments should be allotted to these and other misdemeanours. In the table below, views on

Views on parents' and children's influence on punishments

What say should parents and children have in the kinds of punishment that are used in school?

	At least some say[1] %	**Little or no say** %
Parents should have	86	14
Children should have	61	38

[1] This includes the responses of young people who selected the options 'all of the say' and 'quite a bit of the say' and 'some of the say'.

the respective weighting of parental and student opinions on this subject are set alongside each other.

Young people see a strong role for their parents and, to a lesser extent, for themselves in setting patterns of maintenance of discipline. There was no sense of unrealistic power-seeking on the part of the respondents, although there were some variations related to gender, age and race.

- Girls (66%) were more likely to suggest that children have a say (includes 'all of the say', 'quite a bit of the say' and 'some of the say') in determining school punishments than boys (57%).
- The older the respondent, the less inclined was he or she to ascribe a role to the child.

There was little variation in response according to social class or household composition.

In the 1994 survey, the views of adults on this matter were also sought and 66% thought that parents should have quite a bit of the say in what punishments were used, which did not quite correspond with the young people's views.

Conclusion

The data presented in this chapter suggest that:

- Young people believe strongly that parents should make an input into determining the curriculum; they also feel that children and young people themselves should have a say.
- Examinations were considered by young people as a sound means of determining ability; however, it was considered important that due weight also be given to classroom assessment.
- Young people indicated that in their view, publishing examination results has a value, although publishing primary school test results is not seen to be so important.
- Issues of behaviour — bullying, threats to teachers, drug usage — are acknowledged by young people, and they believe that these should be dealt with seriously. They appear to treat them on a sliding scale of gravity, with bullying least and drug use most serious.

Clearly the role of education as a means of ensuring a good future was highly valued, and school experience represents an important dimension of the lives of young people. There was no impression from the survey that this experience was depressing or negative, but certain problems were acknowledged, particularly in relation to behaviour. Given that adolescents' views are often thought of as ambivalent, subject to frequent change and certainly not homogeneous, the agreement observed on this important subject is interesting.

Determination of curriculum provoked interesting views; it needs to be remembered that it is only in very recent years that this provision in the Education Act 1944 was amended. In that Act, the only required curriculum area was religious education. What went on behind the classroom door was largely the responsibility of the individual teacher. Since the coming of the national curriculum and Education 5 to 14, there now exists in the UK an open framework, with the result that parents, children and young people can reasonably expect the delivery of an explicit content in education, such as has existed in many European countries for some time. Although educational interests including teachers have contributed significantly to this curriculum, it needs to be remembered that they too are obliged and constrained by this, and have no day-to-day say in determining the framework. We can only speculate on the respective weight that teachers would have given to the views of themselves, parents and children on determination of curriculum content. What we do have is a strongly expressed view that parents and young people should have a say. By implication we mean 'more say', because at present they have very little.

However, we come back to asking what 'say'? Do we just mean that they should be consulted, or that they have a distinctive contribution to curriculum formation which must be accommodated? On what aspects of the curriculum should parents and young people comment, or do we just want them to be more visible in the process? If they are to become involved in curriculum content determination, would it be accepted that they have the competence and expertise to do so?

The matter of sex education highlights an important need, and the actual weight and importance given to sex education in school is very much determined by politics and ideology. What we have here is young people's own views and we gain an impression that they are very much influenced by the transitional stage in which they find themselves; they do not think it so important that younger children should have sex education — it is a teenage problem in their eyes.

It appears that confidence is expressed in the system of assessing competence, ability and achievement. The young people responded that examinations were valid as a means of determining ability. They also believe strongly in the value of continuous assessment, and perhaps a supplementary question needs to be asked about how to reconcile these views. The re-affirmation of examinations at secondary school level coincides with something of a kickback in higher education, in which the move towards continuous assessment and away from examination has been to some extent arrested. The importance of publishing examination results also highlights confidence in market forces as a means of ensuring quality.

Young people take seriously matters of behaviour and discipline. This is a highly charged area, one in which government has taken substantial action in recent years: it has produced significant guidelines in the shape of *Achieving Good Behaviour in Schools* (OFSTED, 1993), it has re-instituted data collection on exclusion, and it has undertaken campaigns including one to counteract bullying in school. Young people too want their say: is this reasonable and realistic? Does it represent dissatisfaction with school? On the face of it, the respondents were not overwhelmed by the problems of behaviour and disorder and there was a strong sense that they wished established order to be reinforced — behaviour disorder should be taken seriously, and it should be controlled, punished and dealt with.

The attitude of young people to the school experience was constructive, informative and helpful. They rely on the maintenance of aspects of the system which could be regarded as conservative, and the indications are that any suggestions which they may have on improvement would be moderate and realistic.

References

Allen, I. (1987), *Education in Sex and Personal Relationships*, London: Policy Studies Institute.

Cohen, R., Hughes, M. with Ashworth, L. and Blair, M. (1994), *School's Out: The family perspective on school exclusion*, London: Family Service Units and Barnardo's.

Elton Report, the (1989), *Discipline in Schools*. London: HMSO.

Family Planning Association (1994), *Young People's Attitudes towards Sex Education*, London: FPA.

Halsey, A.H. (1991), 'Failing education', in Jowell, R., Brook, L., Taylor, B. with Prior, G. (eds), *British Social Attitudes: the 8th report*, Aldershot: Dartmouth.

Halsey, A.H. and Lievesley, D. (1994), 'Education: reaction to reform', in Jowell, R., Curtice, J., Brook, L. and Ahrendt, D. (eds), *British Social Attitudes: the 11th Report*, Aldershot: Dartmouth.

Johnson, A.M., Wadsworth, J., Wellings, K. and Field, J. (1994), *Sexual Attitudes and Lifestyles*, Oxford: Blackwell Scientific.

Kingman, S. (1994), 'United against bullying', *Health Education*, **2**, March: 18–20.

Mellor, A. (1990), *Bullying in Scottish Secondary Schools, Spotlight 23*. Edinburgh: SCRE.

Oakley, A., Fullerton, D., Holland, J., Arnold, S., France-Dawson, M., Kelley, P. and McGrellis, S. (1995), 'Sexual health education interventions for young people: a methodological review', *British Medical Journal*, **310**, 158–62.

OFSTED (1993), *Achieving Good Behaviour in Schools*, London: HMSO.

O'Moore, A.M. and Hillery, B. (1989), 'Bullying in Dublin schools', *Irish Journal of Psychology*, **10**, 426–41.

Parker, H. and Measham, F. (1994), 'Pick 'n mix: changing patterns of illicit drug use amongst 1990s adolescents', *Drugs Education Prevention and Policy*, **1**, 1: 5–13.

Shaw, C. (1994a), *Changing lives 1*, London: Policy Studies Institute.

Shaw, C. (1994b), *Changing lives 2*, London: Policy Studies Institute.

Shaw, C. (1994c), *Changing lives 3*, London: Policy Studies Institute.

Skinner, A. (1992), *Bullying: an annotated bibliography of literature resources.* National Youth Bureau: Youth Work Press.

Smith, P.K. (1991), 'The silent nightmare: bullying and victimisation in school peer groups', *The Psychologist*, **4**: 243–8 .

Thomson, R. with Scott, L. (1992), *An Enquiry into Sex Education*, London: Sex Education Forum.

United Nations Committee on the Rights of the Child (1995), *Concluding Observations of the Committee on the Rights of the Child: United Kingdom of Great Britain and Northern Ireland*, Geneva: UN Committee report.

Wellings, K., Wadsworth, J., Johnson, A.M., Field, J., Whitaker, L. and Field, B. (1995), 'Provision of sex education and early sexual experience: the relation examined', *British Medical Journal*, **311**: 417–20.

Whitney, I. and Smith, P.K. (1993), 'A survey of the nature and extent of bullying in junior/middle and secondary schools', *Educational Research*, **35**, 1: 3–25.

Wright, D.J. and Pearl, L. (1995), 'Knowledge and experience of young people regarding drug misuse, 1969–94', *British Medical Journal*, **310**: 20–4.

6 Young people, politics and the media

DAVID WALKER

Conventional wisdom says young people are uninterested. "For this generation politics has become a dirty word", opine Wilkinson and Mulgan (1995). The evidence seems to support the cliché. The *Guardian* (June 19, 1995, Second Front p.2) reported the results of Brighton District Council's sample survey of 16–19-year-olds: "Only one respondent out of 385 said that politics were important to them." The British Youth Council found a fifth of 16–25-year-olds were not registered to vote, four times as many as in any other age group (British Youth Council, 1993).

Is this picture repeated in what the evidence from the *Young People's Social Attitudes* (YPSA) *Survey* shows of young people's political affiliations? This chapter asks what young people can know of politics, given their use of potential sources of information, notably the mass media. Behind that lies a broader query which cannot be satisfied here. It is whether there is some cognitive minimum necessary for political consciousness. Do young people know enough about happening events, personalities and institutions to 'be political'? Or does their use of media (or, as some might prefer to put it, their use by media) indicate that they simply cannot know enough to be political? Let's make the assumption — some might find it heroic — that the media are adequate carriers of political knowledge. The resulting proposition might be: young people cannot do politics because they do not read newspapers, and behind that the causal proposition: because they do not want the kinds of (political) information which newspapers, even the tabloids, tend to purvey.

Does this reflect some deep-seated shift in values or is the lack of interest of young people in politics a phenomenon of the life cycle? Hitherto, there has been a rough positive correlation of age and political participation, at least from young adulthood through to retirement. Conventional wisdom suggests that when people get mortgages and children and their patterns of employment stabilize, their material interests propel them into more active political participation, either to defend their interests or to seek redress for evident disparities in biographies and life chances. Some suggest there is evidence of a once-for-all change in disposition, that we are witnessing 'individualization'. Young people's use of the mass media and their responses to inquiries such as this one about their degree of political interest show a marked turn away from the 'public space' which may parallel the movement away from people's self-identification through employment towards the creation of identities through leisure, gender and so on. The implication — especially worrying for parties of the Left — is that some kind of 'privatization' of political attitudes is occurring.

But already this is to apostrophize 'young people' as if they existed as more than a statistical artefact, as if they were a cultural formation in the terms expressed by Roger Daltrey ("talking 'bout my generation"). And that is to beg a question.

A general election will be held in 1997 if not before, and that fact explains why attention is currently being paid to the political affinities of young people — why, on the Left at least, people who till recently thought Blur was a regional pronunciation of the Labour leader's name have applied themselves to the pop music charts. The parties know that relatively few of the 16–25 age group vote, and that playing the youth card could alienate older voters. But it is not just the votes of young people the parties are after. There is a kind of renewal by association. The relative attractiveness of the parties to younger people is a symbol that party leaders are themselves in some cultural or psychological sense youthful, supple, energetic and that remains a welcome quality in an ageing society.

So the parties spend time devising formulae that might induce first-time voters (who could currently be as young as 16) to answer Labour or Tory or Liberal Democrat or nationalist when questioned by pollsters. It is, however, a relatively unrewarding and possibly dangerous business. The propensity to vote among 18–25-year-olds is less than for most others up to the middle elderly (Wilkinson and Mulgan, 1995). Policies tailored to win an endorsement by 'youth' could offend the aged; the Liberal Democrats recently backtracked swiftly from policy commitments on the legalization of controlled drugs when it was realized this show of liberalism might offend older party supporters. That was exceptional. By and large in Britain inter-generational politics is noticeable by its absence. Commentators, overly influenced by US developments, strive to discern the beginnings of inter-generational conflict over paying for pensions (Johnson *et al.*, 1989). The fact is that there has never yet been a great debate over the merits of educational (youth) versus social security (the aged) spending couched in age-specific terms. That does not preclude age variations of attitude towards, say, responsibility for providing post-retirement income. There is evidence that 'Thatcher's children' have taken on board the message that state provision for their own old age may be insufficient though the actual take-up of personal pension schemes among younger adults suggests a gulf, which the operation of compound interest will only widen, between the pension-haves and the pension have-nots of the fourth and fifth decades of the century to come.

Attention also gets paid to the political behaviour of young people (that is to say its absence) because of unease on the part of their elders that they have in some sense gone to the bad. On the Left, this may be a fear that Thatcher's children are the avatars of a permanently altered state of political awareness; they will carry market individualism and suspicion of collective purposes in politics into the far future; they will never know nor want to know what a trade union is. On the Right, the amoralism of youth threatens anarchy. Young antinomianism is as disturbing to the advocates of market liberalism as young materialism is welcome.

Such fear of the future of present-day youth may or may not be groundless. In the here-and-now of party politics youth is not an interest group worth palliating because it threatens no political retribution. It has no collective political identity and the youth vote is unlikely to make much difference at the general election. But that is not the end of the story. Both party politicians and the rest of us are perennially anxious about the succeeding generation; signs and symbols of its alienation or 'unfitness' cause alarm. Voting, or the stated intention to prefer one party over another at the polls, is political behaviour that can be measured and appraised. A more intriguing concept is that of political consciousness — how far people are mental participants in political argument, whether or not they take part in formal politics by voting or joining parties or interest groups. If political consciousness is undergoing some long-term shift, it will show up in today's young people.

Political identification

Let us focus, first, on two questions. What does the cohort in the YPSA survey say about its political identification, at least in terms of conventional party politics? What do we know about its ingestion of the basic factual information, from the printed and broadcast media, that arguably is the only basis of political consciousness, whether that is expressed in attachment to parties, single-issue campaigns or in other ways?

The survey immediately confirms that politics is a minority pursuit among young people. Overt identification with party is limited, with only 21% of the sample assenting to the idea they 'support' a particular party. Yet there are also signs that 'interest in politics' is still regarded by young people as a culturally approved thing, something they should at least parrot (see table on opposite page). So more than half the sample expressed some interest, even if not very much in 'what is going on in politics'. Outright lack of interest ('none at all' in answer to the question of how much interest they have in politics) was the response of 27%. Old stereotypes about politics existing in a public realm where men feel more at home than women get some support from the data. Proportionately more women express political indifference. Nearly 43% of young men versus just over 34% of young women acknowledged 'some' or 'a lot' or 'a great deal' of interest in politics.

Level of interest in politics

How much interest do you generally have in what is going on in politics?

	Females	**Males**	**All**
	%	%	%
A great deal	3	3	3
Quite a lot	8	11	9
Some	23	29	26
Not very much	35	26	32
None at all	29	26	27

Are these findings about degrees of political interest worrying? No: democracy can surely still prosper when less than a third of the adult population-to-be is 'uninterested' in politics. When two-thirds of young people admit to some, even if small, interest there is political (collective) life in the old dog yet. That 32% answer the question about political interest with 'not very much' could be interpreted positively, provided it contains sufficient space for occasional voting, or attending a protest meeting or, at the very least, refusing the opinion pollster's offer of the 'don't know' column.

There is a generational nostrum about youth tending to be left-leaning and radical, usually based more on the public identification of certain performers who appeal to young people with radical and/or left-of-centre causes. At the last general election a majority of those aged under 25 who voted, voted Conservative. In the YPSA survey, in tune with the political mood of the moment, the Labour Party picks up the sample's stated preference: 35% answer Labour when prodded into making a party commitment. The Tories (14%), the Liberal Democrats (10%) and the Greens (6%) fall in conventional order, with the Don't Knows on 24%.

Party affiliation, for the affiliated, does not seem to be strong. Of those expressing a preference, 19% agreed their support was 'fairly strong', whereas 42% gave the sample equivalent of a shoulder-shrug, answering 'not very strong'. Should we interpret that pessimistically? Hair-shirt democrats with visions of Athenian hillsides crowded with the (male and non-slave) population might deplore the fact that those figures imply that only a small core of people will ever be actively involved. The potential base for party membership is slim. Optimists might observe that party membership has always been a minority pursuit and only an (erroneous) theory of history has propagated the idea that entire social formations could or should get inside the party walls. Spread through the population, 'strong' supporters totalling a fifth of those expressing a party preference could be enough of a leaven to ensure the democratic loaf gets baked.

This — expected — picture of a largely apolitical or uninterested majority of young people seems to cohere with the group's consumption of mass media. That word 'consumption' is of course pejorative. It begs any number of questions about how people use, or are used by newspapers and television. We know very little in detail about reading and viewing, in terms of their effect upon consciousness. What we can identify, in this survey, is the pattern of readership among young people. Under half the sample (45%) normally reads a daily morning newspaper at least three times a week; over half (55%) does not. As with political interest, there is a small though noticeable gender difference: fewer young women than young men say they are regular newspaper readers. Some 59% of young women say they do not read a newspaper. The responses of young male and female respondents to the question of newspaper readership are tabulated below.

Gender and newspaper reading habits

Do you normally read any daily morning newspaper at least 3 times a week?

	Females	Males	All
	%	%	%
Yes	41	50	45
No	59	50	55

Newspaper reading can be presented in this way: newspapers that are broadly speaking in the political centre or on the Left attract about 13% of the entire sample; newspapers of the Right (excluding *Today*, the affiliation of which at the time of writing was unclear) attract just under 27%. That Left/Right disproportion does not of course hold just for young people; it is a fact of British political culture (Curran and Seaton, 1991), and we need to bear in mind, of course, that most young people do not 'choose' their newspapers. They simply read the paper that their parents get. It means that when they read political opinions and often enough political reportage, a majority of readers gets a right-of-centre view. What we do not know is how far that translates into political behaviour or consciousness. If, as some people suggest, the political partisanship of newspapers has increased in recent years, does that imply the 'political socialization' of young people coming into adulthood in the mid to late nineteen-nineties will have a rightwards orientation?

Political knowledge

If we sought to draw up some kind of 'cognitive balance sheet' for political knowledge and information for young people, we would naturally look to sources of fact and comment other than the newspapers (and note how little we know about their interaction). Television and radio news and current affairs, and documentary programming, is clearly such a source. People learn things at second hand. Conversation in the peer group, in the family, at work, at leisure is another source. Context may affect the credibility of the information; what people hear in pubs may influence more than what is read or viewed. We know little about the credibility of messages passed at home, between the genders, or between the generations.

Educational institutions are another obvious source of information, at least for that growing fraction of the youth age group attending them after the minimum leaving age, though contemporary civic information may not figure as such on the syllabus of further or higher education courses. We should not ignore factual and political information contained in programmes and media labelled entertainment. Soap opera may — if the media debates about story-lines in various soaps does indeed reflect what people say — change consciousness and may even influence public policy and judges' decisions. Information is contained in games offered for play on home computers, and on systems to which computers give access. Nonetheless, certain kinds of political information remain a specialty of the newspapers, particularly policies in contention between the parties.

Take for example the issue of a state-regulated minimum wage. Debate is currently fierce. Many economists, employers' organizations and commentators argue a minimum wage would, by increasing the price of labour, cut demand and exacerbate unemployment. Others, citing empirical evidence, suggest that the supply and demand effects in real labour markets are not so direct; the personal and collective benefits of a minimum wage outweigh the costs. It is not easy to adjudicate. Yet entrants to the labour market — young people — would be likely to be among those receiving a minimum wage. As an interest group they would be active participants in discussion. But to take part in debate they need facts. To get facts they would need to read newspapers, the only mass medium which provides sufficient detail.

But what if, as the survey evidence suggests, they are not reading newspapers or rather are reading newspapers where coverage of the minimum wage is likely to be scanty or slanted? Nearly 82% of the sample either read newspapers of the right or are non-readers. That could mean, on this issue at least, the 'cognitive disenfranchisement' of four-fifths of young people. To a cold-eyed party strategist wondering what issues to make prominent in forthcoming campaigns, this conclusion might have significance. It might imply that policy on the minimum wage would inevitably be made 'above the heads' of the mass of those allegedly to benefit from it; they would be unlikely to thank the authors of any new policy. Are such calculations ever made as rationally as that implies? We might conclude that here is an instance of policy — and there are many others — that is in fact 'owned' by those unlikely themselves to be affected by it and a matter of indifference or ignorance to those likely to be affected by it.

Does television not offer an alternative source of political information, which given the nature of British broadcasting is likely to be unbiased? In general, television tends to be information-poor, unfocussed and unspecialized. Even a prestige television news bulletin such as the BBC Nine O'Clock News provides only capsule accounts of complex issues — such as the minimum wage — as opposed to news events. Even if television were a fuller source of political information, we know its use is age-related; time spent watching television is at a maximum among 12–15-year-olds but drops off in the later teenage years.

Radio is another potential source. Even channels dedicated to entertainment, such as BBC Radio One, provide a diet of fact and argument, and not just in news bulletins. According to unpublished BBC surveys, the likes and dislikes among young people for types of information closely follow those of the population at large. News about health is deemed most interesting; news about business and local government least. The age profile for those programmes, such as BBC Radio Four's Today programme, which do seem to set agendas and shape issues is markedly older; Radio Five Live does not have much of a following among those under 20.

Does all this suggest that young people are, politically speaking, 'ignorant'? The media supply information, and may determine the limits of our knowledge of events and their causes. Should we infer then that without the media there is no public opinion … given their relationship with the media, there is no such thing as youth opinion, because they do not know enough to have firm views? It could of course be argued that ignorance, if not actually bliss, is not antagonistic to the operations of democracy and representative politics. Sir Robert Peel's famous aphorism about public opinion being a compound of folly and newspaper paragraphs did not prevent his joining the side of the electoral reformers in 1832 — even if ignorant public opinion had to be served. There is much evidence of low levels of political information in the USA but that is compatible with relatively high levels of political participation. Leichter (1994) discusses interesting experiments such as that in Oregon where citizens gave intelligible responses to a difficult question — how to ration expensive medical treatment. Cynics and Aristotelians might observe that democracy depends on the non-participation of the majority, making their ignorance of political detail functional.

Another, more original argument might be that contemporary ignorance is the ante-chamber to future political change. Reforming organizations such as Charter 88 are anxious to combat the idea that young people's knowledge of political facts implies their approval of the institutional *status quo* (Charter 88, 1995). Put another way, lack of knowledge of how despised institutions work could be an indicator of desire for change. This would imply young people were, as it were, candidates for alternatives. The trouble with this argument of course is that knowledge of alternatives has to come from somewhere, especially if the alternative involves complex reformation of the state or fiscal redistribution in the name, say, of environmental protection or sustainability.

The survey data are ambiguous. Although young people may not read newspapers they do seem one way or another to have secured some basic but important political facts. Presented with a series of propositions in quiz format, the sample answered pretty accurately, identifying the Prime Minister, the President of the USA and getting some constitutional facts broadly right. Eighty per cent agreed that the Tory Party had won the last election and 76% agreed that Northern Ireland was part of the United Kingdom. That there are separate elections for the UK and European Parliaments was known by 65%. These may be simple propositions but the accuracy of the response suggests basic information does get ingested, whatever the source.

Conclusion

Are we right to conclude from the survey that there is a 'deficit' in young people's knowledge, even if they do know something about institutions and personalities and are capable of conceptualizing change? The implication behind that question is that democracy depends on identifiable quanta of knowledge, and that knowledge and participation are related. Much of the literature on young people and the media has an anxious tone from Himmelweit *et al.* (1958) to Wartella (1995). It may reflect age-old preoccupations. Parents and possessors of cultural authority have always tended to fear the up-coming generation is deficient, unworthy of assuming its obligations. History shows that things are usually all right on the night and succeeding generations tend to be remarkably similar to their parents in most respects.

Yet that could sound complacent. Although we have to accept that, "the history of mass communication is conspicuously lacking in any clear evidence on the precise influence of the mass media" (Cumberbatch and Howitt, 1989), that need not inhibit a more discursive conclusion about trends in media content and use. Back to the example of the minimum wage. It surely matters, in representative politics, if large interest groups are excluded (or exclude themselves) from policy discussion. Policy becomes the preserve of a class of policy-makers, likely to be uninformed by direct experience. Or a case for policy change may go unmade because the relevant interest group does not exercise itself. Wilkinson and Mulgan (1995) are the latest of a series of authors to suggest that young people may have absorbed more detached and reserved attitudes to the political system: the evidence is the declining membership of collective institutions such as trade unions and political parties. Alternatively, this may be a 'realistic' outlook, reflecting a rational assessment of the limits of government and the utility of participation. In terms of the minimum wage example, young people care to seek no information about minimum wage policy because they have already written off government as an effective agency in their lives. They prefer to read newspapers of the right or not to read at all because of their prior judgement about the political process and its possible outcomes.

What we know from trade surveys and the like is that young people are active media users, capable of making discrete choices among periodicals and programming. The 'cognitive balance' discussed earlier is a product of choice not manipulation.

A conclusion that suggested young people do have political consciousness and it is critical of existing party political set-ups is likely to be welcomed by those who assert that among young age groups party politics is giving way to various kinds of public action through single-issue events and organizations. Young people know 'enough' in other words to reject political parties and join Greenpeace. But this survey makes such a conclusion doubtful. What kind of political consciousness can it be that is so under-informed? Public action, especially that taking place outside the conventional boundaries of political parties, requires more not less political fact and knowledge. Political action is surely dependent on fact-formed consciousness. The problem the YPSA survey leaves us with is where those facts come from.

References

British Youth Council (1993), *Young People: Changing the Face of British Politics*, Briefing Paper, London: British Youth Council.

Charter 88 (1995), *A Parliament for our Times*, Schools'Pack, London: Charter 88.

Cumberbatch, G. and Howitt, D. (1989), *A Measure of Uncertainty: the effects of the mass media*, London: John Libbey.

Curran, J. and Seaton, J. (1991), *Power without Responsibility: the Press and Broadcasting in Britain*, (4th edn), London: Routledge.

Himmelweit, H.T., Oppenheim, A.N. and Vince, P. (1958), *Television and the Child: An empirical study of the effects of television on the young*, London: Oxford University Press.

Johnson, P., Conrad, C. and Thomson, D. (1989) *Workers versus Pensioners: Intergenerational Justice in an Ageing World*, Manchester: Manchester University Press.

Leichter, H. (1994), 'Democratic Cures: the Lessons from Oregon' in *Demos Quarterly,* Issue 3, London: Demos.

Wartella, E. (1995), 'Media and Problem Behaviours in Young People', in Rutter, M. and Smith, D. (eds), *Psychosocial Disorders in Young People*, London: John Wiley.

Wilkinson, H. and Mulgan, G. (1995), *Freedom's Children. Work, relationships and politics for 18–34 year olds in Britain today*, Paper No 17, London: Demos.

7 'It wasn't like this in our day': young people, religion and right and wrong

HELEN ROBERTS

For many centuries, the condition, probity and honesty of the young have been preoccupations of the not-so-young. Young people are never quite as good as we were when we were young, never quite as attentive at school, as obedient to their parents, as law-abiding or as honest. Their pastimes are less desirable than ours, their morals more suspect. This is not a new concern. Peter the Hermit in the eleventh century suggested that "the world is passing through troubled times. The young people have no reverence for their parents ...". Even then, it was an ancient grievance. In the first century BC, the poet Horace described the man who was "a praiser of past times when he was a boy, a castigator and censor of the young generation."

What evidence we have suggests that some of the wilder fears about young people are exaggerated. Recent reviews (e.g., Rutter and Smith, 1995) point to important changes in moral values over the last half-century, but doubt whether there is evidence of a general moral decline. What light is cast on this by the findings of the *Young People's Social Attitudes* (YPSA) *Survey*?

Other chapters indicate that the stereotype of the young as a monstrous army at odds with their families, the institutions of the state and the world at large is not borne out by the attitudes expressed in this survey. But in terms of probity and honesty, what does the survey show? And what does it tell us about the attitudes children and young people have to religious beliefs, or to the expression of these through formalized religion and churchgoing?

This chapter describes two sets of data which we explored in the YPSA survey. The first deals with attitudes to churchgoing and religious beliefs, the second with attitudes to a set of specific questions about some everyday moral dilemmas.

Children, young people and religion

One of the traditional forms of moral influence on the young is religion. As Peter Brierley has pointed out, 'religious statistics are intrinsically fascinating. They are more than a codifying of an interesting sociological phenomenon. They reflect in numerical terms a … pattern of human behaviour, belief and understanding." (Brierley, 1988: 518). In a society such as contemporary Britain, where there are people with one of many religions, or with none, the links between religion and morality are complex. But it remains pertinent to enquire into them, not only because for many people they are intertwined, but because much public discussion of morality uses religious points of reference. Meanwhile, religious bodies continue to express a concern for both the moral and material state of the nation in the light of their own beliefs about obligation and responsibility. Religious comments on a wide range of issues of social concern are part of the fabric of society's debate about its present condition. A recent report from the Church of England Board for Social Responsibility suggests that much of society's concern about family life focuses on the way in which young people are perceived as being delinquent, promiscuous and beyond their parents' control (Working Party of the Board for Social Responsibility, 1995: 198). A submission to the working party from the Centre for Policy on Ageing indicated the part that religion plays in the lives of some: "Religion is for some older people one of the most enduring features of their inner world, sustaining them through the difficulties that can be experienced in later life." Does religion have a similarly important part to play at the other end of the life cycle?

Spiritual concern for the young, is a feature of all religions. A Jewish prayer draws attention to the responsibilities of adults to provide a secure framework within which children can flourish. Part of the 'Selichot', the prayers for forgiveness reads:

> *"For the sin we have committed in leaving our groping children*
> *To wander young and alone in the wilderness*
> *Without guidance, without faith, to seek their own God*
> *For all these, O God of forgiveness, forgive us, pardon us, grant us remission."*

Whatever notions about the secularization of society may be current, any examination of social attitudes must recognize the widespread, varied, and deeply rooted place of religion. From the start, the *British Social Attitudes* (BSA) *Survey* has asked a set of questions on religious affiliation and religious practice. Although the 'decline' of religion over the last 200 years is frequently taken for granted, there is some evidence that this view may be over-pessimistic, that there have been rises as well as declines, and that the Victorian age of faith has more reality in subsequent imaginings than in contemporary reality (Harris, 1993: 150ff.). In the 9th BSA report, Greeley suggests that "the existence of [a] golden age is usually assumed rather than proven" and draws attention to recent evidence suggesting that even in the high Middle Ages, religious devotion may not have been as common as is sometimes thought. He cites the work of Finke and Stark (1992), reporting that in 1738, 30 Oxfordshire parishes reported only a combined average total of 911 communicants on the four great festivals of Christmas, Easter, Whitsun and Ascension. Greeley concludes that, "the British are more religious than they think they are … they are also more religious than they used to be." (Greeley, 1992: 52, 69).

Meanwhile, membership of non-Christian groups increased from around 800 000 in 1975 to over a million in 1980, owing mainly to a 50% increase in the number of Muslims. There were significant increases in the number of Hindus and Sikhs over the same period (Ramprakash, 1986, reported in Furnham and Gunter, 1989) and there are thought to have been substantial further increases since then.

In the YPSA survey, we asked three questions related to religion. The first was whether young people saw themselves as belonging to a religion. The second explored religious practice, and asked whether, apart from weddings, baptisms and funerals, they went to services or meetings connected with their religion. The final question in this section shows how young people responded when faced with a set of possible statements about belief in God ranging from 'I don't believe in God and I never have' to 'I believe in God now and I always have.'

The first point to emerge is that for the young people in the YPSA survey, religion is not the taboo subject it is sometimes felt to be. Whether or not politics and religion are thought in some quarters to lie outside the pale of polite discussion, our respondents clearly felt no such inhibition. Indeed, young people were rather clearer on what they thought of God and religion than on what they thought of politics. Although a quarter of young people replied that they did not know how they would vote if a general election were to be held tomorrow, they were more decisive on the subjects of 'belonging' to a religion, churchgoing and belief in God, with only 8% (47) of respondents saying they did not know whether they believed in God. Only one person was unwilling to say whether they 'belonged' to a particular religion, and the 'don't knows' and 'not answered' were in single figures for each of the three questions on religion and belief in God. Young people, therefore, seem willing to say what they think about religion, and to know what they think, or to know well enough to respond to questions about religion in an attitude survey.

We begin this chapter with the response to the question on belief in God, which, on the face of it, is remarkably reassuring for those who fear that young people have no moral anchorage in a religious faith.

By far the largest group (45%) are those who say they believe in God and always have. There is also a substantial minority of converts who believe in God now, but didn't used to. A third of young people say they do not believe in God.

Belief in God

The statement which best describes your beliefs about God:	%
I don't believe in God and I never have	16
I don't believe in God now, but I used to	17
I believe in God now, but I didn't used to	13
I believe in God now, and I always have	45

These beliefs in God, not surprisingly, are related to allegiance to a particular religion. Young people were asked for both their religion, if any, and (among the Christians) for their denomination. Nine per cent (52) identified themselves as Christian, but with no denomination, and 15% (89) as Church of England. Fifty-four per cent of young people (315) — a rather larger proportion than those who do not believe in God — say that they do not consider that they belong to a particular religion. It is difficult to know just what this answer means. Does it mean, for instance, that they have no closer relationship with Christianity than, say, Buddhism? And given that some of the young people who do not feel they belong to a religion say they believe in God, what consequences does their belief have for them?

The table below excludes religions or denominations mentioned by fewer than 20 respondents; the full list may be found in the questionnaire given in the appendix.

Belonging to a particular religion

	%
No religion	54
Christian (no denomination)	9
Roman Catholic	9
Church of England/Anglican	15
Islam/Muslim	3

It is no news that the relationship between churchgoing, and belief in God, is complex, and so our survey showed. Even of those who believe in God, not all find formal observance congenial. A submission from Mencap to the Church of England's Board for Social Responsibility's report on families in Church and society pointed out: "Nothing is more off-putting than a church which seems to have the motto: 'Come unto me, all ye that are heavy laden, but only if ye fit.'" (Working Party of the Church of England Board of Social Responsibility, 1995).

Of those professing a belief in the YPSA survey, only 12% (68) went to church (or a religious service) once or more a week, and 16% of believers (93) went to church never, or practically never.

Age and gender in religion

Greeley (1992) has pointed out that we know that religious adherence, religious observance and churchgoing vary with age. Research on religion and the lifecycle from the USA for instance, indicates that religious faith and observance begin to decline in the middle teens, and reach bottom in the middle twenties. Only 10% of women aged 70 or over, and 20% of men of the same age have no religious affiliation.

Less is known about beliefs in the young. The years covered by YPSA (12–19) cover a span of huge transition in a young person's life. Were there differences between different age groups in religious adherence, observance of belief in God? And were there differences by gender?

In terms of gender, differences were similar to those found in adults. Girls and young women were more likely to profess a belief than boys and young men. Sixty-one per cent of males and 48% of females do not regard themselves as belonging to a particular religion. However, they do sometimes go to religious services, apart from weddings funerals and baptisms. Only 13% of boys and young men, and 19% of girls and young women never, or practically never, attend a service or a meeting connected with their religion. Fifty-six per cent of males and 61% of females said they 'believed in God'.

Selecting appropriate age bands was difficult. As Chapter 1 describes, there are no clear lines of demarcation between the state of childhood and that of young adulthood. We selected age bands that enabled us to look at children and young people who were still part of the compulsory school system (12–15), those on the verge of young adulthood (16–17) and those who were legally adults (18–19). There was not a great deal of difference in terms of the age bands in those claiming not to belong to a particular religion. Age bands are similarly lacking in importance when describing

Church attendance, or belief in God. Once again, there is a disparity between the 'belief in God' question and belonging to a particular religion, which is presumably accounted for by those who believe in God, but do not see themselves as allied to a particular group.

Age and religious beliefs and observances

		Age	
	12–15	**16–17**	**18–19**
	%	%	%
No religion	52	63	53
Attend religious meeting or ceremony at least once a year	28	21	32
Believe in God[1]	62	52	55

[1] This includes responses from young people who selected the options 'I believe in God now, but I didn't used to' or 'I believe in God now and I always have'.

Household type

While we cannot claim that our survey data cast light on whether the family that prays together stays together (or *vice versa*), and although the numbers living independently are too small for generalization, our data do not appear to lend support to those who view some kinds of household or family structure as more godly than others. The answers given reveal that there is no consistent hierarchy of households in terms of godliness. Young people living outside the family home have the lowest percentage of 'no religion' responses, but they also have the lowest propensity to express a belief in God. Forty per cent of respondents living away from their family households (who will of course be on average older than the sample as a whole) claimed 'no religion' in comparison with more than half of respondents in households with one or two parents, as the table below shows. When it came to churchgoing, however, those from more traditional households were more likely to be church attenders. We find less variation in the answers to the question of whether the respondent believed in God — a slightly different issue from that of being adherent to a particular religion.

Household type and religious belief and observances

	Household type		
	Independent[1]	One parent	Two parents
	%	%	%
No religion	40 (20)	59	54
Belong to a particular religion	50 (25)	41	45
Attend religious meeting or ceremony at least once a year	20 (10)	23	29
Believe in God[2]	50 (25)	56	60

[1] Numbers (in brackets) as well as percentages are given for the young people in independent households, given the small numbers.
[2] This includes responses from young people who selected the options 'I believe in God now, but I didn't used to' or 'I believe in God now and I always have'.

Children, young people and right and wrong

All major religions make a connection between right and wrong and the way in which one lives one's daily life. But there are ways other than religion in which children and young people learn to make moral choices, and there is, of course, no perfect fit between expressing strong religious or moral beliefs, and acting accordingly. In the BSA 1985 report, Michael Johnston and Douglas Wood wrote of the public scandals of the 1970s which had raised fundamental questions about the rules defining acceptable and unacceptable conduct in Britain (Johnston and Wood, 1985). Like concerns about youth, concerns about probity are no mere transitory phenomenon of the nineties.

We asked a number of questions about apparently simple choices of right and wrong in everyday life, which are summarized below. As in the BSA survey, the low numbers of 'don't knows' and 'not answered' to these questions indicates that the questions were understood, and respondents felt able to make judgements of right and wrong.

Firstly, respondents were asked to reflect on what they might do were they to be presented with an unexpected opportunity to come by £5. The largest proportion would pick it up and keep it. Very few young people said that they were uncertain what they would do. But as the sum increased, the inclination to hang on to it decreased. The response when they were asked sequentially what they would do if they saw £5, £20 or £100 on the pavement are shown in the next table.

Responses to money in the street

Suppose you are alone in an empty street, no-one is likely to come by and see you. There is a note lying on the pavement. Would you …

	£5	**£20**	**£100**
	%	%	%
Leave it there?	5	4	1
Pick it up and hand it in at the police station?	16	38	72
Pick it up and keep it?	77	56	25

In this respect, this situation is the converse of that attributed to George Bernard Shaw at a dinner party where prostitution was the subject of conversation. He asked his neighbour at the dinner table if she would sell herself for £1. Of course, the answer was no. The stakes were upped, and she was asked if she would come away with him to Cannes for £1 million. She agreed that she might. GBS then suggests that they repair immediately to below the table. "What do you think I am Mr Shaw?", "We've established what you are madam, we're just haggling over the price."

Over time, the proportion of adult respondents to the BSA survey saying that they would keep the change for £10 when £5 was proffered has increased, but it is difficult to tell, as Halpern (1995) has pointed out, whether this relates to an increase in dishonesty, or a decrease in the value of £5, thus making it appear a less serious issue. The same problem relates to children and money. Children receive more pocket money than their parents did 20 years ago, though Utting (1995: 10) describes how "two economic recessions in 15 years appear to have left their mark. According to the annual Walls/Gallup survey (Bird's Eye Walls, 1995), the average £2.05 a week pocket money given to children in 1995 is worth 16% more, after allowing for inflation, than in 1975. Yet the purchasing power of pocket money remains below its 1981 peak, when it was worth 38% more in real terms. The latest survey reports a significant fall during the past year alone in children's earnings from Saturday jobs, paper rounds, and other paid work." It is difficult to know from a survey what children and young people make of the value of money, but data available to us, from a study of the aspirations of young people with whom Barnardo's works, indicates a sense, particularly among the older young people, that even £100 does not go very far these days. A 9-year-old in Dundee, asked what he would do with £100 said: "If you gave me £100, I'd laugh. I'd go home with it, and give it to my mum. I'd ask for about a pound, and I'd spend it on juice. I'd tell her I only wanted a pound, I wouldn't want any more. She could have it."

A 17-year-old young offender from Wales said: "If I had £100, I'd spent it on the baby. It's his birthday tomorrow. A hundred pounds doesn't go far with a baby." (Proctor, 1993).

Although for Shaw's dinner party companion, hesitation fell as the price rose, with the young people in the YPSA survey, the higher the sum, the less their apparent inclination to put the cash into their pockets. This points to moral behaviour somewhat tempered by pragmatism — a state not unknown in the public and private behaviour of adults. But it also suggests that young people have a scale of 'wrongness,' and that little sins are more acceptable than big ones.

Age and gender in concepts of right and wrong

Is this desire to 'take the money' evenly distributed across young people as a group? Are girls as likely as boys to pocket the cash? And are younger children more or less willing than older ones to hang on to the money?

The responses from girls confirm their known law-abiding tendencies. In every case, girls were more likely than boys to say they would leave the money where it was, more likely to claim they would hand it in to the police, and less likely to admit that they would pick it up and keep it. The shape of the gradient is just as it is for boys — increasing numbers handing the money over as the sum increased. As might be expected, young people felt that they would become rather less inclined to leave the money on the pavement the larger the sum.

Gender responses to finding money in an empty street

	Leave it in the street		Hand it in to the police		Pick it up and keep it	
	Males	Females	Males	Females	Males	Females
	%	%	%	%	%	%
£5	4	7	14	19	81	73
£20	4	5	33	44	61	49
£100	1	2	69	75	27	22

As the sum rose, both boys and girls were more inclined to say that they would hand over the sum to the police, with girls remaining the more likely to give this response.

Although the majority of children and young people would act honestly with the larger sums of money, a substantial minority said they would pick up and keep £20 or £100.

To explore concepts of right and wrong within the context of situations a little more tricky than the note on the pavement, young people were asked to consider a situation where a person is given change for £10 in a shop, when s/he has actually tendered only £5. The first time the question is asked the shop is a 'big store,' the second time 'a corner shop.'

Views on keeping money from a big store

A man gives a £5 note for goods he is buying in a big store. By mistake, he is given change for a £10 note. He notices, but keeps the change. Please say which of the things on the card comes closest to what you think of the situation:

	%
Nothing wrong	6
A bit wrong	35
Wrong	43
Seriously wrong	13
Very seriously wrong	3

It is known that there is a gap between what people feel is right in general, and what they feel is right for them. Asking what an individual might do him or herself, rather than asking what they think is right or wrong in general pushes a question closer to the area of behaviour, which we know has an imperfect association with attitudes. As Furnham and Gunter (1989: 4) point out, frequently attitudes are measured at a very general abstract level, and behaviour at a highly specific level. The more the two are in alignment, the better the one predicts the other.

It can be seen from the table which follows that those who might hang onto the money are not confined to those who think that there would be 'nothing wrong' in doing so. It is clear that quite a number of those who recognize that an action is wrong, will nevertheless undertake it. To that extent, education programmes or 'parenting education' aimed at teaching children the difference between right and wrong may be doomed to failure unless attention is also given to the context and climate within which knowledge about right and wrong will be translated into behaviour.

Individual's actions in a big store

And might you do this [i.e. keep the extra change in a big store] if the situation came up?

	%
Yes	41
No	52
Don't know	6

The questions of what one does in a rather anonymous situation may be different from what one might do in a more parochial or neighbourly context. This was explored using the example of a 'corner shop' rather than a big store. Young people were more likely to consider pocketing the change under these circumstances wrong (see table below), indicating a distinction between some unknown 'other' being harmed, and harm being done in one's own back yard. It might be fanciful to see this as the difference between abstract or universal moral rules, and rules derived from the conventions and conduct of real and familiar communities. Nevertheless, the more immediate wrongs were felt to be the more reprehensible.

Views on keeping money from a corner shop

A man gives a £5 note for goods he is buying in a corner shop. By mistake, he is given change for a £10 note. He notices but keeps the change. Please say which of the things on the card comes closest to what you think of the situation:

	%
Nothing wrong	5
A bit wrong	24
Wrong	48
Seriously wrong	18
Very seriously wrong	5

But even in this 'back yard' situation, quite a number of the young people who believe that in general it is wrong to pocket the wrong change, would themselves do it if the situation came up. Although these findings may show considerable honesty in the answering of questionnaires, they also indicate that young people may be able to put their scruples to one side when the opportunity arises.

Individual's actions in a corner shop

And might you do this [i.e. keep the change in a corner shop] if the situation came up?

	%
Yes	28
No	68

That people are apparently less likely to think it wrong to pocket money belonging to larger, anonymous bodies is a finding consistent with other studies, and is presumably bad news for banks, supermarkets, and large concerns. Although people are more inclined to feel that they themselves would be honest when given too much change in a corner shop, more than a quarter still admit to thinking they might hang onto the money in these circumstances.

These figures do not, of course, tell us whether or not people are dishonest. They simply tell us what people say they feel about dishonesty in particular situations, and what they say they might do themselves when faced with making a moral choice.

Does honesty go up or down with age? We know that young people frequently 'grow out' of petty crime, and our data do not enable us to comment on the honesty of respondents, but dividing them into three groups of 12–15-year-olds, 16–17-year-olds and 18–19-year-olds, the answers on all of the questions about finding cash, or keeping change showed scant variation.

Conclusion

In 1994, questions on right and wrong in private life were not among those asked of adults, so we are not able to compare what children and young people say with responses from adults in the same year, and we believe it could be unsafe to compare children and young people in 1994 with adults some years ago. This is one of the areas where trend data will make the survey increasingly useful, as we see how (or whether) the responses of young people to questions such as these change over time, and how close they are to the answers to the same questions asked of adults.

Ironically, we have more data enabling us to study over time the opinions expressed by adults about the morals and the conduct of the young than we do about the realities of young people's own social attitudes and actions. The current survey may contribute to modifying wilder claims in a number of directions, but its full potential must wait upon the collection of data covering a number of years in future reports.

References

Bird's Eye Walls (1995), *The Walls Monitor 1995*, London: Walls.

Brierley, P. (1988), 'Religion', in Halsey, A.H. (ed.), *British Social Trends since 1900: A guide to the changing social structure of Britain*, Basingstoke: Macmillan.

Finke, R. and Starke, R. (1992), *The Churching of America: Winners and Losers in Our Religious Economy*, New Brunswick: Rutgers University Press.

Furnham, A. and Gunter, B. (1989), *The Anatomy of Adolescence: Young people's social attitudes in Britain*, London: Routledge.

Greeley, A. (1992), Religion in Britain, Ireland and the USA, in Jowell, R., Brook, L., Prior, G. and Taylor B. (1992), *British Social Attitudes, the 9th Report*, Aldershot: Dartmouth.

Halpern, D. (1995), 'Values, Moral and Modernity: the Values, Constraints and Norms of European Youth', in Rutter, M. and Smith, D. (eds), *Psychosocial disorders in young people*, Chichester: John Wiley.

Harris, J. (1993), *Private Lives, Public Spirit: Britain 1870–1914*, Harmondsworth: Penguin.

Johnston, M. and Wood, D. (1985), 'Right and wrong in public and private life', in Jowell, R. and Witherspoon, S. (eds), *British Social Attitudes, the 1985 Report*, Aldershot: Gower.

Proctor, J. (1993), Research report and interview findings for McNeish, D. and Parish, A., *Look Who's Talking*, Barkingside: Barnardo's.

Ramprakash, D. (1986), *Social Trends No 16*, London: HMSO.

Rutter, M. and Smith, D. (eds) (1995), *Psychosocial disorders in young people*, Chichester: John Wiley.

Utting, D. (1995), 'Changing childhood: For better or worse?', in *The Facts of Life*, Barkingside: Barnardo's.

Working Party of the Church of England Board for Social Responsibility (1995), *Something to Celebrate: Valuing Families in Church and Society*, London: Church House Publishing.

Appendix I
Technical details of the survey

ALISON PARK

British Social Attitudes and Young People's Social Attitudes

The *British Social Attitudes* (BSA) *Survey* is a nationwide annual survey carried out by Social and Community Planning Research (SCPR). In 1994, 3469 people aged 18 or over were interviewed. Three versions of the questionnaire were used, each consisting of a series of question 'modules' dealing with a variety of topics. Some modules were asked of the full sample and others were asked of a random two-thirds or one-third of the sample.[1]

In 1994, for the first time, the survey was supplemented by the *Young People's Social Attitudes* (YPSA) *Survey*. All young people aged 12–19 who lived in the same household as a BSA respondent were eligible for interview.

Sample design

The BSA survey is designed to yield a representative sample of adults aged 18 or over. The sampling frame for the 1994 survey was the Postcode Address File (PAF), a list of addresses (or postal delivery points) compiled by the Post Office.

For practical reasons, the sample is confined to those living in private households. People living in institutions (though not in private households at such institutions) are excluded, as are households whose addresses were not on the Postcode Address File.

The sampling method for adults involved a multi-stage design, with three separate stages of selection.

Selection of sectors

At the first stage, postcode sectors were selected systematically from a list of all postal sectors in Great Britain. Before selection, any sectors with fewer

1. For further details, see Jowell, R., Curtice, J., Park, A., Brook, L. and Ahrendt, D. (eds) (1995), *British Social Attitudes: the 12th report*, Aldershot: Dartmouth.

than 500 addresses were identified and grouped together with an adjacent sector; in Scotland all sectors north of the Caledonian Canal were deleted (because of the prohibitive costs of interviewing there). Sectors were then stratified on the basis of:

- Registrar General's Standard Region
- Population density (persons per hectare) with variable banding used according to region, in order to create three equal-sized strata per region
- Ranking by percentage of homes that were owner-occupied, from the 1991 Census figures.

Two hundred postcode sectors were selected, with the probability of their selection being proportional to the number of addresses in each sector. In other words, a sector with a large number of addresses had a higher chance of being selected than a sector with fewer addresses.

Selection of addresses

Thirty addresses were selected in each of the 200 sectors. The sample was therefore 200 × 30 = 6000 addresses, selected by starting from a random point on the list of addresses for each sector, and choosing each address at a fixed interval. The fixed interval was calculated for each sector in order to generate the correct number of addresses. At this point, each address was randomly allocated a number corresponding to one of the three versions of the questionnaire.

When selecting addresses, we took account of the fact that some addresses have more than one dwelling unit (for example, a tenement building or a house that has been converted into self-contained flats).[1] This information can be gleaned from the Multiple-Output Indicator (MOI) which is available through PAF. In cases where the MOI indicated that there was more than one dwelling unit at an address, the chances of the given address being selected from the list of addresses was increased so that it matched the total number of accommodation spaces. As would be expected, the vast majority (99.2%) of MOIs had a value of one.

1. In many cases a dwelling unit will comprise one household. However, this is not necessarily the case — a dwelling unit may contain more than one household.

Selection of individuals

Interviewers called at each selected address and listed everyone who was eligible for inclusion in the sample — that is, all persons currently aged 18 or over and resident at the selected address. The interviewer then, if necessary, used random selection procedures to select one person for interview. Where there were two or more households or 'dwelling units' at the selected address, interviewers first had to use random methods to select one household or dwelling unit.

Selection of young people

All young people aged 12–19 who lived in the same household as an adult respondent were eligible for interview.

Weighting

To ensure unbiased estimates, data had to be weighted to compensate for the selection procedures used to obtain the sample. As discussed above, not all the units covered in the BSA survey (from which the YPSA sample was derived) had the same probability of selection. The weighting for the YPSA data takes into account the different chances of selection which occurred at address level and household level.[1]

All weights fell within a range between 0.125 and 3. The vast majority of cases had a weight of 1.000. The weighted sample was scaled to make the number of weighted productive cases exactly equal to the number of unweighted productive cases (*n*=580). The following distribution of weights was used:

Weight	No.	%	Scaled weight
0.125	2	0.3	0.125
0.333	2	0.3	0.334
0.500	4	0.7	0.501
0.750	1	0.2	0.752
1.000	569	98.1	1.002
3.000	2	0.3	3.007

All the figures presented in this report are based on weighted data.

1. For further information about weighting, see Lynn, P. and Lievesley, D. (1991), *Drawing General Population Samples in Great Britain*, SCPR: London.

Fieldwork

A small-scale pilot survey was carried out in late March 1994 in order to test question wording, questionnaire structure and flow.

Interviewing on the main survey was mainly carried out during May, June and July 1994, with a small number of interviews taking place until October.

Fieldwork was conducted by interviewers drawn from SCPR's regular panel. All interviewers attended a one-day briefing conference to familiarize them with the selection procedures used and the content and structure of the questionnaire.

Interviews for the YPSA survey were carried out by the same interviewers who worked on the adult BSA survey. After the interview with the adult in the household, the interviewer established the number of eligible young people living in the household (that is, the number of young people aged between 12 and 19) and, where appropriate, asked permission from a responsible adult to interview them. In most cases the interviewer had to return to the household on at least one occasion.

From a total of 3469 adult interviews, 735 young people were identified as being eligible for interview. The response achieved was as follows:

	No.	**%**
In scope (12–19-year-old in household)	735	100
Interview achieved	580	79
Interview not achieved	155	21
Refused[1]	116	16
Non-contact[2]	17	2
Other non-response[3]	22	3

[1] 'Refusals' comprise refusal by the selected young person, 'proxy' refusals (on their behalf) and broken appointments after which the selected young person could not be recontacted.
[2] 'Non-contacts' comprise cases where the young person could not be contacted (never found at home, on holiday, in hospital, and so on).
[3] 'Other non-response' comprises cases where the young person was incapacitated or ill at home during the survey period, 'partial' interviews (interviews cut short before a specific point in the questionnaire) and any remaining cases which do not fit into either the refusal or non-contact categories outlined above.

The average interview length was 31 minutes.

As mentioned previously, all young people in a household were eligible for inclusion in the survey. The number of households in which one, and more than one, young person was interviewed was as follows:

No. of young people interviewed in household	No. of households	% of sample
1	290	50.0
2	106	36.5
3	23	11.9
4	1	0.7
5	1	0.9

The questionnaire

Approximately half the questions in the YPSA questionnaire were also asked (using exactly the same wording) on one, two or all three versions of the BSA survey. For these questions, then, the answers given by young people (their responses) can be compared to those given by adults. In addition, more detailed comparisons can be made of the responses of young people and those of the adult BSA respondent living in the same household. As some questions were asked of only a third or two-thirds of the adult sample, such comparisons are limited to these specific adults and the young people in their households.

The remaining questions were unique to the YPSA survey and covered issues of special relevance to young people.

Topics covered in the YPSA survey were as follows:

- 'Age of consent' questions
- Judgements of right and wrong
- Education, school life and sex education
- Fear and experience of crime
- Crime and punishment
- Gender roles and family life
- Racial prejudice and discrimination
- Political knowledge, political interest and party identity
- Important factors in 'doing well in life'
- Life ambitions and aspirations.

A number of demographic and other classificatory questions were also included (such as age, sex, religion, current activity and educational experience and expectations). Other background variables (such as those used to derive socio-economic grade) had been included in the adult BSA questionnaire and so were not fielded again in the YPSA questionnaire.

Once the questionnaire was completed, interviewers were asked to indicate whether anyone else had been partially or wholly present during the interview. Responses to this question, perhaps unsurprisingly, varied according to the age of the young person and are shown below. Response did not vary according to the sex of the young person.

		Age of young person		
Presence of other person during interview:	**All** %	**12–13** %	**14–15** %	**16–19** %
Yes, throughout	35.0	43.9	30.7	31.6
Yes, partially	22.4	25.5	22.9	19.7
No	40.6	28.5	43.6	48.2

A copy of the young people's questionnaire, with the percentage distribution of responses added, follows. Percentages are based, unless otherwise specified, on the total weighted sample.

The percentage distributions do not necessarily add up to 100 because of weighting and rounding, or for one or more of the following reasons:

(i) Some sub-questions are filtered — that is, they are asked of only a proportion of respondents. In these cases the percentages add up (approximately) to the proportions who were asked them. Where, however, a *series* of questions is filtered, we have indicated the weighted base at the beginning of that series and throughout have derived percentages from that base.

(ii) If fewer than 50 respondents (unweighted) are asked a question, frequencies (the *number* of people giving each response) are shown, rather than percentages.

(iii) At a few questions, respondents were invited to give more than one answer and so percentages may add to well over 100%. These are clearly marked by interviewer instructions on the questionnaires.

(iv) No percentages are given for statement b), question 43. This is because the statement, one of a series designed to assess political knowledge, concerned John Smith's leadership of the Labour Party and John Smith died at the at the start of our fieldwork period.

LONDON EC1V 0AX Tel: 071-250 1866 Fax: 071-250 1524
SCPR SOCIAL AND COMMUNITY PLANNING RESEARCH
BRENTWOOD, ESSEX CM14 4LX Tel: 0277 200600 Fax: 0277 214117

P.1345 Spring 1994

BRITISH SOCIAL ATTITUDES: 1994

YOUNG PEOPLE'S SURVEY

OFFICE USE ONLY		
8-13		Spare
14-15	4 1	Card no.
16		Spare
25-29		Batch no.

INTERVIEWER TO ENTER		
1-5	6	Serial no.
6-7		Person no.
17-20	0	Sampling point
21-24		Interviewer number

Barnardos
POLICY AND DEVELOPMENT UNIT

n = 580

SECTION A

1. At what age do <u>you</u> think people <u>should</u> be allowed to ...

READ OUT a.- i. AND WRITE IN AGE

a.	... vote in a general election?	MEDIAN:	18
			%
		(Any age/whenever ready)	1.2
		(Don't know)	2.6
b.	... leave home?	MEDIAN:	16
			%
		Any age/whenever ready	8.6
		(Don't know)	1.4
c.	... drive a car on a public road?	MEDIAN:	17
			%
		(Any age/whenever ready)	1.0
		(Don't know)	0.7

And at what age do <u>you</u> think people <u>should</u> be allowed to ... READ OUT...

d.	... see <u>any</u> film they want in a cinema?	MEDIAN:	16
			%
		(Any age/whenever ready)	5.4
		(Other answer)	0.2
		(Don't know)	2.4
		(Not answered)	0.2
e.	... leave school?	MEDIAN:	16
			%
		(Any age/whenever ready)	3.6
		(Don't know)	0.2
f.	... have sex?	MEDIAN:	16
			%
		(Any age/whenever ready)	6.9
		(Other answer)	0.3
		(Don't know)	5.2
		(Not answered)	0.5

OFFICE USE ONLY

n = 580

And at what age do <u>you</u> think people <u>should</u> be allowed to ... READ OUT...

g. ... get married?

MEDIAN:	18
	%
(Any age/whenever ready)	7.4
(Don't know)	2.1

h. ... babysit a child of five for an evening?

MEDIAN:	15
	%
(Any age/whenever ready)	2.6
(Don't know)	0.3

i. ... get a regular part-time job?

MEDIAN:	15
(Any age/whenever ready)	1.8
(Don't know)	0.7

j. ... buy alcohol?

MEDIAN:	18
	%
(Any age/whenever ready)	0.3
(Don't know)	1.0

k. ... be left on their own for an evening?

MEDIAN:	14
	%
(Any age/whenever ready)	3.5
(Don't know)	1.2

SECTION B

2a. Suppose you are alone in an empty street, no-one is likely to come by and see you. There is a £5 note lying on the pavement. Would you ... READ OUT ...

	%
... leave it there,	5.0
pick it up and hand it in at the police station,	16.0
or, pick it up and keep it?	77.1
(Other answer)	0.2
(Don't know)	1.7

OFFICE USE ONLY

n = 580

2b. Suppose it was a £20 note lying there. What would you do... READ OUT...

	%
... leave it there,	4.3
pick it up and hand it in at the police station,	37.5
or, pick it up and keep it?	55.9
(Don't know)	2.2

c. And suppose it was £100 in notes lying there. Would you ... READ OUT ...

	%
... leave it there,	1.4
pick it up and hand it in at the police station,	71.5
or, pick it up and keep it?	25.0
(Other answer)	0.2
(Don't know)	1.9

CARD A

3a. A man gives a £5 note for goods he is buying in a big store. By mistake, he is given change for a <u>£10</u> note. He notices but keeps the change. Please say which of the things on the card comes closest to what you think of this situation?

	%
Nothing wrong	5.6
A bit wrong	34.9
Wrong	43.1
Seriously wrong	12.7
Very seriously wrong	3.1
(Don't know)	0.3
(Not answered)	0.2

b. And might you do this if the situation came up?

	%
Yes	40.8
No	52.1
(Don't know)	6.0
(Not answered)	1.0

CARD A AGAIN

4a. A man gives a £5 note for goods he is buying in a <u>corner shop</u>. By mistake, he is given change for a <u>£10</u> note. He notices but keeps the change. Please say which of the things on the card comes closest to what you think of this situation?

	%
Nothing wrong	4.7
A bit wrong	23.9
Wrong	47.8
Seriously wrong	18.3
Very seriously wrong	5.0

n = 580

4b. And might you do this if the situation came up?

	%
Yes	27.6
No	67.6
(Don't know)	4.4
(Not answered)	0.3

SECTION C

5a. It is now compulsory for state secondary schools to publish their exam results. How useful do you think this information is for parents of present or future pupils? Is it ... READ OUT...

	%
... very useful,	29.7
quite useful,	49.9
or, not really useful?	17.2
(Don't know)	3.1
(Not answered)	0.2

b. And how useful do you think it would be if schools for children aged between seven and eleven published their test results? Would it be ... **READ OUT...**

	%
... very useful,	11.8
quite useful,	37.4
or, not really useful?	47.7
(Don't know)	3.1

CARD B

6a. How much say should parents have in what is taught in schools? Please choose an answer from this card.

	%
All of the say	6.5
Quite a bit of the say	38.6
Some of the say	47.0
Not very much say	4.9
No say at all	2.4
(Don't know)	0.5
(Not answered)	0.2

CARD B AGAIN

b. And how much say should parents have in the kinds of punishment that are used in schools? Please choose an answer from this card.

	%
All of the say	18.4
Quite a bit of the say	36.2
Some of the say	31.4
Not very much say	8.8
No say at all	4.7
(Don't know)	0.5

ONLY

n = 580

CARD B AGAIN

7a. How much say should children have in what is taught in schools? Please choose an answer from this card.

	%
All of the say	6.7
Quite a bit of the say	26.8
Some of the say	40.8
Not very much say	16.7
No say at all	7.6
(Don't know)	1.2
(Not answered)	0.2

CARD B AGAIN

b. And how much say should children have in the kinds of punishment that are used in schools? Please choose an answer from this card.

	%
All of the say	7.4
Quite a bit of the say	18.0
Some of the say	35.4
Not very much say	23.0
No say at all	15.4
(Don't know)	0.3
(Not answered)	0.3

CARD C

8. Which of the following statements comes closest to your views about what kind of secondary school children should go to?

	%
Children should go to a different kind of secondary school, according to how well they do at primary school	30.0
All children should go to the same kind of secondary school, no matter how well or badly they do at primary school	67.2
(Don't know)	2.1
(Not answered)	0.7

9a. Some people think that all schools should teach sex education to children before they are 11. Others say that parents should be allowed to choose whether or not their young child has sex education. What about you? Do you think that ... **READ OUT ...**

	%
... all children aged 11 and under should have sex education at school,	36.7
or, should parents be allowed to choose?	61.2
(Don't know)	1.7
(Not answered)	0.3

IF PARENTAL CHOICE AT a. (CODE 2) OR DK (CODE 8)

b. What about children aged 12 to 16? Do you think that ... **READ OUT ...**

	%
... all children aged 12 to 16 should have sex education at school,	52.6
or, should parents be allowed to choose?	9.0
(Don't know)	0.9
(Not answered)	0.9

OFFICE USE ONLY

n = 580

ASK ALL
CARD D

10. Please tell me, from this card, how much you agree or disagree with each of these statements about <u>secondary schooling</u>.

READ OUT a.- d. AND CODE ONE FOR EACH		Agree strongly	Agree	Neither agree nor disagree	Disagree	Disagree strongly	(Don't know)	(NA)
a. Formal exams are the best way of judging the ability of pupils	%	6.1	39.3	14.1	32.2	6.2	1.6	0.5
b. On the whole, pupils are too young when they have to decide which subjects to specialise in	%	6.3	35.8	18.1	35.1	2.2	1.9	0.5
c. The present law allows pupils to leave school when they are too young	%	2.6	18.5	13.5	57.3	4.9	2.8	0.5
d. So much attention is given to exam results in Britain that a pupil's everyday classroom work counts for too little	%	11.2	52.3	12.2	20.2	0.7	2.9	0.5

11. Can I just check, are you presently at school or sixth form college?

	%
Yes, school	71.2
Yes, sixth form college	8.1
No	20.0
(Not answered)	0.7

PRESENT TENSE IF AT SCHOOL/6TH FORM COLLEGE (CODE 1 OR 2 AT Q.11)
PAST TENSE IF NOT AT SCHOOL/6TH FORM COLLEGE (CODE 3 AT Q.11)

12a. Thinking of your current (*most recent*) school/6th form college. Would you say that <u>students</u> get (*got*) bullied by other students ... **READ OUT ...**

	%
... a lot,	27.2
a little,	54.4
or, not at all?	17.1
(Don't know)	0.7
(Not answered)	0.5

b. And what do you think should happen to someone who <u>keeps on</u> bullying other students at school? Should they be ... **READ OUT ...**

	%
... expelled from their school,	30.7
suspended from their school for some time,	25.8
or, should they be dealt with in some other way but stay at their school?	40.7
Other (WRITE IN)________	1.4
(Don't know)	0.9
(Not answered)	0.5

PRESENT TENSE IF AT SCHOOL/6TH FORM COLLEGE (CODE 1 OR 2 AT Q.11)
PAST TENSE IF NOT AT SCHOOL/6TH FORM COLLEGE (CODE 3 AT Q.11)

13a. Would you say that <u>teachers</u> get (*got*) threatened by students ... **READ OUT ...**

	%
... a lot,	10.6
a little,	39.9
or, not at all?	46.2
(Don't know)	2.5
(Not answered)	0.7

OFFICE USE ONLY

n = 580

13b. And what do you think should happen to someone who <u>keeps on</u> threatening a teacher at school? Should they be ... **READ OUT ...**

	%
... expelled from their school,	53.1
suspended from their school for some time,	23.7
or, should they be dealt with in some other way but stay at their school?	20.5
Other (WRITE IN)________	1.2
(Don't know)	1.0
(Not answered)	0.5

PRESENT TENSE IF AT SCHOOL/6TH FORM COLLEGE (CODE 1 OR 2 AT Q.11)
PAST TENSE IF NOT AT SCHOOL/6TH FORM COLLEGE (CODE 3 AT Q.11)

14a. Would you say that students having drugs in your school happens (*happened*) ... **READ OUT ...**

	%
... a lot,	19.4
a little,	46.5
or, not at all?	28.9
(Don't know)	4.8
(Not answered)	0.5

b. And what do you think should happen to someone who <u>keeps on</u> having drugs in school? Should they be ... **READ OUT ...**

	%
... expelled from their school,	54.6
suspended from their school for some time,	14.3
or, should they be dealt with in some other way but stay at their school?	28.8
Other (WRITE IN)________	1.4
(Don't know)	0.5
(Not answered)	0.5

SECTION D

ASK ALL

Now some questions about crime.

15a. Do you ever worry about the possibility that you or anyone else who lives with you might be the victim of crime?

	%
Yes	61.8
No	37.8
(Not answered)	0.3

IF 'YES' AT a.

b. Is this ... **READ OUT ...**

	%
... a big worry,	10.1
a bit of a worry,	35.1
or, an occasional doubt?	16.2
(Not answered)	0.3

n=580

ASK ALL

CARD E

16. Here are some things that some people do to avoid crime. Which of these do <u>you</u> do? Please give me the number or numbers on the card.

CODE ALL THAT APPLY

	%
I am careful to lock up our home (and/or car)	71.6
I don't go out <u>alone</u>	20.4
I don't answer the door	10.9
I avoid going out at certain times	33.2
I avoid going to certain places	53.0
I avoid public transport	6.0
I carry a personal alarm or a weapon	5.7
I make sure other people in the family take precautions	20.1
None	6.2
Other (**WRITE IN**)________	3.3
(Don't know)	0.2
(Not answered)	0.3

ASK ALL

And now some questions about crimes that may have happened to you.
[NOTE THAT TWO OR MORE CRIMES MAY HAVE HAPPENED ON THE SAME OCCASION]

17. Have you yourself <u>ever</u>...

READ OUT a.- g. AND CODE ONE FOR EACH		Yes	No	No car/bike	(Don't know)	(NA)
a. ... been physically attacked?	%	16.3	83.4		-	0.3
b. ... been threatened?	%	32.6	67.0		-	0.3
c. ... had your home burgled?	%	17.5	81.2		1.0	0.3
d. ... had a car belonging to you or your family stolen or things stolen from a car?	%	45.0	50.8	2.0	1.6	0.7
e. ... had your home or car damaged by vandals?	%	38.6	59.7		1.0	0.7
f. ... had your bike stolen or damaged by vandals?	%	24.2	70.0	5.5	-	0.3
g. ... had something else stolen?	%	30.7	67.8		1.0	0.5

18. **INTERVIEWER: CODE FROM Q.17**

	%
If victim of any crime **(CODE 1 AT ANY Q.17a.-g.)**	82.0
If 'no'/'don't know' to all **(CODE 2,3 OR 8 AT Q17a.-g.)**	17.7
(Not answered)	0.3

IF 'VICTIM OF ANY CRIME' AT Q.18

19a. Do you think that as a result of any of these experiences you are now more <u>aware</u> of crime, or has it made no difference?

	%
More aware	54.0
No difference	27.2
(Not answered)	1.2

ONLY

n=580

IF YES AT a.

19b. And has it actually made you more <u>afraid</u> of crime?

	%
Yes	21.7
No	31.2
(Don't know)	1.0
(Not answered)	1.2

ASK ALL
CARD F

20a. And do you know personally <u>anyone else</u> who has experienced any of these crimes? You needn't tell me which crimes.

	%
Yes	87.5
No	11.5
(Don't know)	0.7
(Not answered)	0.3

IF YES AT a. (CODE 1)

b. Has knowing about someone else's experience of crime made <u>you</u> more <u>aware</u> of crime or has it made no difference?

	%
More aware	59.9
No difference	26.7
(Don't know)	0.5
(Not answered)	1.4

IF MORE AWARE AT b. (CODE 1)

c. And has it actually made <u>you</u> more <u>afraid</u> of crime?

	%
Yes	27.8
No	30.8
(Don't know)	1.2
(Not answered)	1.9

ASK ALL

21. How safe do you feel walking alone in this area after dark ... **READ OUT** ...

	%
... very safe,	14.1
fairly safe,	42.9
a bit unsafe,	28.4
or, very unsafe?	7.8
(Never walk alone)	6.0
(Don't know)	0.3
(Not answered)	0.3

n = 580

OFFICE USE ONLY

SECTION E

22a. Suppose two people - one white, one black - each appear in court, charged with a crime they did not commit. What do you think their chances are of being found guilty? **READ OUT ...**

	%
... the white person is more likely to be found guilty,	3.1
they have the same chance,	48.1
or, the black person is more likely to be found guilty?	43.5
(Don't know)	5.0
(Not answered)	0.3

b. Now suppose another two people from different back- one rich, one poor - each appear in court, charged with a crime they did not commit. What do you think their chances are of being found guilty? **READ OUT ...**

	%
... the rich person is more likely to be found guilty,	3.1
they have the same chance,	30.2
or, the poor person is more likely to be found guilty?	64.4
(Don't know)	1.9
(Not answered)	0.3

c. Now suppose another two people - one British and one Irish - each appear in court, charged with a burglary they did not commit. What do you think their chances are of being found guilty? **READ OUT ...**

	%
... the British person is more likely to be found guilty,	2.2
they have the same chance,	66.7
or, the Irish person is more likely to be found guilty?	25.7
(Other answer)	0.2
(Don't know)	4.7
(Not answered)	0.5

CARD G

23. Here are some possible ways of helping to prevent crime in Britain. How effective do you think each one is?

READ OUT a. - g. AND CODE ONE FOR EACH		Very effective	Quite effective	Not very effective	Not at all effective	(Don't know)	(NA)
a. Less violence and crime on television	%	11.4	39.5	38.5	8.9	1.4	0.3
b. People taking religion more seriously	%	6.4	25.5	46.9	18.8	2.0	0.3
c. Sending more people to prison	%	17.4	41.9	30.3	8.0	2.1	0.3
d. Sending fewer people to prison	%	1.9	16.5	49.3	28.0	4.0	0.3
e. Firmer discipline in families	%	24.5	53.6	14.8	4.1	2.2	0.7
f. Stricter discipline in schools	%	21.5	56.4	18.5	2.3	0.9	0.3
g. Reducing poverty	%	27.8	48.9	14.3	3.8	4.7	0.5

n = 580

OFFICE USE ONLY

CARD H

24. Suppose someone under 16 commits a burglary for the first time. How much are you in favour or against each of the following ways of dealing with them?

READ OUT a.- d. AND CODE ONE FOR EACH		Strongly in favour	In favour	Neither favour nor against	Against	Strongly against	(Don't know)	(NA)
a. Give them a strong warning but leave them to their parents to sort out	%	14.6	38.3	16.2	25.4	4.9	0.3	0.3
b. Make them spend a certain amount of time helping people in the community	%	18.3	62.3	8.6	8.2	1.4	0.7	0.5
c. Send them to a special institution for young criminals	%	8.8	25.7	18.7	37.1	7.6	1.6	0.5
d. Send them to an ordinary prison for adult criminals	%	4.1	5.5	8.3	42.9	37.8	1.0	0.3

CARD I

25. And, in your opinion, which of these would be the best way of dealing with someone under 16 who commits a burglary for the first time. Please choose one answer from this card.

CODE ONE ONLY

	%
Give them a strong warning but leave them to their parents to sort out	26.6
Make them spend a certain amount of time helping people in the community	49.5
Send them to a special institution for young criminals	20.6
Send them to an ordinary prison for adult criminals	2.2
Other (**WRITE IN**) ______	0.3
(Don't know)	0.3
(Not answered)	0.3

CARD J

26. Do you think British courts should be able to sentence murderers to death or not? Please choose your answer from this card.

CODE ONE ONLY

	%
Definitely	34.3
Probably	29.6
Probably not	15.8
Definitely not	17.1
(Don't know)	2.8
(Not answered)	0.3

SECTION F

n = 580

CARD K

27. Please choose a number from this card to say how much you agree or disagree with each of these statements.

	READ OUT a.- c. AND CODE ONE FOR EACH		Agree Strongly	Agree	Neither agree nor disagree	Disagree	Disagree strongly	(Don't know)	(NA)
a.	A working mother can establish just as warm and secure a relationship with her child as a mother who does not work	%	17.4	51.5	12.6	15.0	1.4	1.6	0.5
b.	All in all, family life suffers when the woman has a full-time job	%	2.4	26.3	22.5	38.7	7.8	1.7	0.5
c.	Having a job is the best way for a woman to be an independent person	%	10.0	51.2	23.7	11.4	0.5	2.6	0.5

CARD K AGAIN

28. And how much do you agree or disagree with these statements. Please choose a number from the card.

	READ OUT a.- c. AND CODE ONE FOR EACH		Agree Strongly	Agree	Neither agree nor disagree	Disagree	Disagree strongly	(Don't know)	(NA)
a.	A man's job is to earn money; a woman's job is to look after the home and family	%	2.6	7.8	11.0	41.9	35.7	0.5	0.5
b.	It is not good if the man stays at home and cares for the children and the woman goes out to work	%	2.1	11.8	20.0	49.8	15.8	-	0.5
c.	Family life often suffers because men concentrate too much on their work	%	5.6	38.1	27.1	23.6	2.5	2.6	0.5

n = 580

CARD K AGAIN

29. Still looking at this card, please choose a number to show how much you agree or disagree with these statements.

	READ OUT a. - e. AND CODE ONE FOR EACH		Agree Strongly	Agree	Neither agree nor disagree	Disagree	Disagree strongly	(Don't know)	(NA)
a.	It is better to have a bad marriage than no marriage at all	%	1.0	5.8	7.6	57.3	26.2	1.2	0.9
b.	One parent can bring up a child as well as two parents	%	10.8	44.5	16.4	23.2	3.4	0.9	0.9
c.	It is all right for a couple to live together without intending to get married	%	17.6	62.1	10.5	7.3	1.0	0.5	0.9
d.	It's a good idea for a couple who intend to get married to live together first	%	23.6	58.4	10.9	4.5	0.5	1.2	0.9
e.	When there are children in the family, parents should stay together even if they don't get along	%	2.6	14.7	21.1	46.8	12.0	1.9	0.9

CARD L

30. I am going to read out jobs people can do. Looking at this card, please say for each job whether you think it is particularly suitable for men, particularly suitable for women, or suitable for both men and women equally.

	READ OUT a. - h. AND CODE ONE FOR EACH		Particularly suitable for men	Particularly suitable for women	Suitable for both equally	(Don't know)	(NA)
a.	Police officer	%	15.6	0.3	83.6	-	0.5
b.	Secretary	%	0.3	44.2	54.8	0.2	0.5
c.	Car mechanic	%	42.3	0.3	56.7	-	0.7
d.	Nurse	%	0.2	18.3	80.5	0.2	0.9
e.	Bank manager	%	9.7	0.9	88.9	-	0.5
f.	Family doctor/GP	%	4.0	3.2	92.3	-	0.5
g.	Member of Parliament	%	7.8	1.4	89.3	1.0	0.5
h.	Airline pilot	%	29.2	1.4	68.5	0.2	0.7

OFFICE USE ONLY

n=580

CARD M

31. Imagine a man and woman who are living together. I would like to ask you some questions about how you think they should share family jobs. Please choose an answer from this card to show who you think should...

	READ OUT a. - f. AND CODE ONE FOR EACH		Mainly the woman	Mainly the man	Shared equally	(Don't know)	(NA)
a.	... shop for groceries?	%	18.8	1.6	79.1	-	0.5
b.	... make the evening meal?	%	16.4	1.7	81.0	0.3	0.5
c.	... do the washing and ironing?	%	20.6	0.9	77.0	0.9	0.7
d.	... make small repairs around the home?	%	2.0	51.7	45.3	0.5	0.5
e.	... look after sick family members?	%	22.7	0.7	75.8	0.2	0.7
f.	... organise the family's money and payment of bills?	%	8.6	11.4	79.0	0.5	0.5

32. At what age do you think young people should be expected to...

PLEASE ENTER AGE IN BOX FOR a. & b. OR CODE (Don't know)
READ OUT a. AND b. AND WRITE IN AGE

a. ... help with the daily washing up? MEDIAN: 10

	%
(Other answer)	0.9
(Don't know)	4.7
(Not answered)	0.5

b. ... regularly make their own bed? MEDIAN: 9

	%
(Other answer)	1.0
(Don't know)	2.6
(Not answered)	0.5

SECTION G

CARD N

33. To which of these groups do you consider you belong?

CODE ONE ONLY

		%
Black:	of **African** or **Caribbean** or **other** origin	1.0
Asian:	of **Indian** origin	1.9
	of **Pakistani** origin	2.9
	of **Bangladeshi** origin	-
	of **Chinese** origin	-
	of **other** origin (**WRITE IN**) ______	0.7
White:	of **British** origin	89.6
	of **Irish** origin	0.3
	of **other** origin (**WRITE IN**) ______	1.7
Mixed origin:	(**PLEASE SAY WHICH**) ______	1.2
	(Refused)	-

OFFICE USE ONLY

n=580

Now I would like to ask you some questions about racial prejudice in Britain.

34a. Firstly, thinking of Asians - that is, people whose families were originally from India, Pakistan and Bangladesh - who now live in Britain. Do you think there is a lot of prejudice against them in Britain nowadays, a little or hardly any?

	%
A lot	50.8
A little	41.1
Hardly any	6.1
(Don't know)	1.2
(Not answered)	0.9

b. And black people - that is, people whose families were originally from the West Indies or Africa - who now live in Britain. Do you think there is a lot of prejudice against them in Britain nowadays, a little or hardly any?

	%
A lot	39.0
A little	48.6
Hardly any	10.0
(Don't know)	1.6
(Not answered)	0.9

c. Do you think there will be more, less or about the same amount of racial prejudice in Britain in 5 years time compared with now?

	%
More in 5 years	24.9
Less	35.1
About the same	36.1
Other answer (**WRITE IN**) ______	0.2
(Don't know)	2.6
(Not answered)	1.2

35. How would you describe yourself ... **READ OUT** ...

	%
... as very prejudiced against people of other races,	2.2
a little prejudiced,	25.8
or, not prejudiced at all?	70.4
Other answer (**WRITE IN**) ______	0.2
(Don't know)	0.5
(Not answered)	0.9

36a. On the whole, do you think people of Asian origin are not given jobs these days because of their race ... **READ OUT** ...

	%
... a lot,	17.2
a little,	49.6
or - hardly at all?	27.7
(Don't know)	4.7
(Not answered)	0.9

n = 580

36b. And on the whole, do you think people of West Indian origin are not given jobs these days because of their race ... **READ OUT** ...

	%
... a lot,	16.1
a little,	50.1
or - hardly at all?	27.4
(Don't know)	5.5
(Not answered)	0.9

37. There is a law in Britain against racial discrimination, that is against giving unfair preference to a particular race in housing, jobs and so on. Do you generally support or oppose the idea of a law for this purpose?

	%
Support	75.4
Oppose	13.6
(Don't know)	10.0
(Not answered)	1.0

38. **INTERVIEWER TO CODE FROM Q.33:**

Respondent is white (CODE 07, 08, or 09)	1	ASK Q.39
Respondent is Asian (CODES 02 - 06)	2	GO TO Q.40
Respondent is black (CODE 01)	3	GO TO Q.41
Other (CODES 10 OR 97)	4	GO TO Q.42

IF CODE 1 AT Q.38

39a. Do you think most white people in Britain would mind or not mind if one of their close relatives were to marry a person of Asian origin?
IF 'WOULD MIND': A lot or a little? RECORD IN COL. a.

b. And you personally? Would you mind or not mind? **IF 'WOULD MIND'**: A lot or a little? **RECORD IN COL. b.**

c. Do you think most white people in Britain would mind or not mind if one of their close relatives were to marry a person of black or West Indian origin?
IF 'WOULD MIND': A lot or a little? **RECORD IN COL. c.**

n = 532

d. And you personally? Would you mind or not mind?
IF 'WOULD MIND': A lot or a little? **RECORD IN COL. d. THEN GO TO Q.42**

	ASIAN ORIGIN		BLACK ORIGIN	
	a. Most people	b. Self	c. Most people	d. Self
	%	%	%	%
Mind a lot	17.3	6.6	14.7	5.1
Mind a little	37.2	10.7	44.2	10.2
Not mind	40.4	80.8	36.8	81.8
Other answer	0.6	0.2	0.6	0.4
(Don't know)	3.8	1.1	2.6	1.1
(Not answered)	0.8	0.6	1.1	1.3

NOW GO TO Q.42

IF CODE 2 AT Q.38

40a. Do you think most Asian people in Britain would mind or not mind if one of their close relatives were to marry a white person?
IF 'WOULD MIND': A lot or a little? RECORD IN COL. a.

b. And you personally? Would you mind or not mind? **IF 'WOULD MIND'**: A lot or a little? **RECORD IN COL. b.**

c. Do you think most Asian people in Britain would mind or not mind if one of their close relatives were to marry a person of black or West Indian origin? **IF 'WOULD MIND'**: A lot or a little? **RECORD IN COL. c.**

n = 32

d. And you personally? Would you mind or not mind?
IF 'WOULD MIND': A lot or a little? **RECORD IN COL. d. THEN GO TO Q.42**

	WHITE		BLACK ORIGIN	
	a. Most people	b. Self	c. Most people	d. Self
	n	n	n	n
Mind a lot	10	1	11	-
Mind a little	17	7	13	10
Not mind	4	22	5	17
Other answer	-	-	1	1
(Don't know)	1	2	1	2
(Not answered)	-	-	1	2

NOW GO TO Q.42

IF CODE 3 AT Q.38

41a. Do you think most black people in Britain would mind or not mind if one of their close relatives were to marry a white person?
IF 'WOULD MIND': A lot or a little? RECORD IN COL. a.

b. And you personally? Would you mind or not mind? **IF 'WOULD MIND'**: A lot or a little? **RECORD IN COL. b.**

c. Do you think most black people in Britain would mind or not mind if one of their close relatives were to marry a person of Asian origin?
IF 'WOULD MIND': A lot or a little? **RECORD IN COL. c.**

n = 6

d. And you personally? Would you mind or not mind?
IF 'WOULD MIND': A lot or a little? **RECORD IN COL. d. THEN GO TO Q.42**

	WHITE		ASIAN ORIGIN	
	a. Most people	b. Self	c. Most people	d. Self
	n	n	n	n
Mind a lot	-	-	-	-
Mind a little	2	-	2	-
Not mind	4	3	2	3
Other answer	-	1	-	1
(Don't know)	-	-	1	-
(Not answered)	-	2	1	2

n=580

OFFICE USE ONLY

SECTION H

ASK ALL

42a. Generally speaking, do you think of yourself as a supporter of any one political party?

	%
Yes	20.6
No	78.2
(Not answered)	1.2

IF NO AT a. (CODE 2)

b. Do you think of yourself as a little closer to one political party than to the others?

	%
Yes	21.8
No	56.4
(Not answered)	1.3

IF NO AT b. (CODE 2)

c. If there were a general election tomorrow, which party would you hope would win? **CODE ONE ONLY UNDER c. & d.**

IF YES (CODE 1) AT a. OR b.

d. Which one? **CODE ONE ONLY UNDER c. & d.**

	%
Conservative	13.8
Labour	34.6
Liberal Democrats	9.7
Scottish Nationalist	3.3
Plaid Cymru	-
Green Party	5.5
Other party (**WRITE IN**) ______	0.6
Other answer (**WRITE IN**) ______	0.3
None	6.4
Refused/unwilling to say	0.9
(Don't know)	23.5
(Not answered)	1.4

IF ANY PARTY CODED AT c. & d., ASK e.

e. Would you call yourself very strong ... (**QUOTE PARTY NAMED**) ... fairly strong, or not very strong?

	%
Very strong	5.3
Fairly strong	18.9
Not very strong	41.5
(Don't know)	1.7
(Not answered)	0.5

ASK ALL

f. How much interest do you generally have in what is going on in politics ... **READ OUT** ...

	%
... a great deal,	2.6
quite a lot,	9.4
some,	26.2
not very much,	32.1
or, none at all?,	27.4
(Don't know)	0.9
(Not answered)	1.4

n=580

OFFICE USE ONLY

43. Here is a quick quiz. For each thing I say, tell me if it is true or false. If you don't know, just say so.
READ OUT a. - k. AND CODE ONE FOR EACH

			True	False	(Don't know)	(NA)
a. John Major is the first British male Prime Minister	*(false)*	%	3.9	90.1	5.2	0.9
b. The leader of the Labour Party is John Smith	*(not asked)*	%	-	-	-	-
c. The number of members of Parliament is about 100	*(false)*	%	29.3	40.7	28.8	1.2
d. The president of the U.S.A is George Bush	*(false)*	%	15.9	77.4	5.9	0.9
e. The longest time allowed between general elections is four years	*(true)*	%	59.0	19.2	20.4	1.4
f. Great Britain is a member of the European Community	*(true)*	%	83.8	4.1	11.1	1.0
g. Britain has separate elections for the European parliament and the the British parliament	*(true)*	%	65.3	7.6	26.3	0.9
h. Northern Ireland is part of the United Kingdom	*(true)*	%	76.1	14.7	8.1	1.0
i. Women are not allowed to sit in the House of Lords	*(false)*	%	16.3	65.5	16.6	1.6
j. The Conservative Party won the last general election	*(true)*	%	79.7	5.6	13.9	0.9
k. The leader of the Conservative party is Margaret Thatcher	*(false)*	%	5.5	86.6	7.0	0.9

CARD O

44. And now some questions about doing well in life. First, how important is coming from a wealthy family? Please choose your answer from this card.

READ OUT a.- e. AND CODE ONE FOR EACH		Essential	Very important	Fairly important	Not very important	Not at all important	(Don't know)	(NA)
a. (Coming from a wealthy family?)	%	2.4	11.1	28.6	43.6	12.9	0.7	0.7
b. Having a good education yourself?	%	25.4	53.7	18.6	1.2	0.3	-	0.7
c. Hard work?	%	20.8	51.2	24.9	1.6	0.2	0.3	1.1
d. And how important is a person's race?	%	1.5	8.7	14.7	38.9	32.8	2.6	0.9
e. Being a man or a woman?	%	0.9	5.0	11.9	36.4	41.6	3.3	0.9

SECTION I

n = 580

45a. Now some more general questions.
Firstly, do you normally read any <u>daily morning</u> newspaper at least 3 times a week?

	%
Yes	44.8
No	54.5
(Not answered)	0.7

IF YES AT a.

b. Which one do you normally read?
IF MORE THAN ONE ASK: Which one do you read most frequently?

ONE CODE ONLY

	%
(Scottish) Daily Express	3.8
Daily Mail	4.7
Daily Mirror/Record	11.2
Daily Star	2.3
The Sun	14.7
Today	0.9
Daily Telegraph	1.3
Financial Times	-
The Guardian	1.0
The Independent	0.7
The Times	0.2
Morning Star	-
Other local paper	1.2
Other national paper	1.9
(More than one paper)	1.0
(Not answered)	0.7

n = 580

ASK ALL

46. Do you regard yourself as belonging to any particular religion?
IF YES: Which?

CODE ONLY ONE - DO NOT PROMPT
BUT PROBE FOR DENOMINATION

	%
No religion	54.3
Christian - no denomination	9.0
Roman Catholic	9.1
Church of England/Anglican	15.3
Baptist	0.9
Methodist	1.0
Presbyterian/Church of Scotland	2.3
Free Presbyterian	-
Brethren	-
United Reform Church (URC)/Congregational	0.2
Other Protestant (WRITE IN) ______	0.3
Other Christian (WRITE IN) ______	0.9
Hindu	0.3
Jewish	-
Islam/Muslim	3.5
Sikh	1.4
Buddhist	0.2
Other non-Christian (WRITE IN) ______	-
(Refused/unwilling to say)	0.2
(Don't know)	0.5
(Not answered)	0.7

IF ANY RELIGION OR DON'T KNOW AT Q.46

47. Apart from such special occasions as weddings, funerals and baptisms, how often nowadays do you attend services or meetings connected with your religion?

PROBE AS NECESSARY
FOR CORRECT PRECODE

	%
Once a week or more	11.8
Less often but at least one in two weeks	2.8
Less often but at least once a month	4.3
Less often but at least twice a year	4.1
Less often but at least once a year	3.7
Less often	1.2
Never or practically never	16.0
Varies too much to say	0.3
Refused/unwilling to answer	-
(Don't know)	0.2
(Not answered)	1.4

OFFICE USE ONLY

n=580

ASK ALL
CARD P

48. Please tell me which of the statements on this card best describes your beliefs about God?

	%
I don't believe in God and I never have	15.7
I don't believe in God now, but I used to	16.9
I believe in God now, but I didn't use to	12.8
I believe in God now and I always have	45.3
(Other answer)	0.2
(Don't know)	8.1
(Not answered)	1.0

49. **CODE SEX OF RESPONDENT**

	%
Male	49.1
Female	48.6
(Not answered)	2.2

50. And now some questions about yourself. First, how old were you last birthday? **WRITE IN:** ☐☐

51a. **INTERVIEWER TO CODE AGE FROM Q.50**

	%
Respondent aged 12 to 15	59.9
Respondent aged 16 to 19	39.5
(Not answered)	0.7

IF AGED 16 TO 19
CARD Q

b. Which of these descriptions applies to what you were doing last week, that is, in the seven days ending last Sunday?
PROBE: Any others?
CODE ALL THAT APPLY IN COLUMN I
IF ONLY ONE CODE AT I, TRANSFER IT TO COLUMN II.
IF MORE THAN ONE CODE AT I, TRANSFER HIGHEST ON LIST TO II.

	Col.I	Col.II
	%	%
In full-time education at school, college, or university	01	23.3
On government training/employment programme	02	2.5
In paid work for at least 10 hours in week	03	7.4
Waiting to take up paid work already accepted	04	0.3
Unemployed and registered at a benefit office	05	2.1
Unemployed, not registered, but actively looking for a job	06	1.2
Unemployed, wanting a job, but not actively looking for a job	07	0.9
Permanently sick or disabled	08	-
Looking after the home	09	1.2
Doing something else (WRITE IN) ______	10	0.5

IF IN PAID WORK (CODE 3 AT Q.51)

52a. In your (main) job are you ... **READ OUT ...**

	%
... an employee,	7.1
or, self-employed?	0.3

OFFICE USE ONLY

n=580

52b. And how many hours a week do you normally work in your (main) job?
(IF RESPONDENT CANNOT ANSWER, ASK ABOUT LAST WEEK)

	%
10 - 15 hours	0.5
16 - 23 hours	0.5
24 - 29 hours	0.3
30 or more hours	6.0
(Don't know)	

ALL

53. **CODE ACTIVITY STATUS FROM Q.50 AND/OR Q.51:**

	%
Respondent aged 12 to 15 or in full-time education (code 1 at Q.50 **OR** code 01 at Q.51)	83.2
Respondent not in full-time education (codes 02 to 10 at Q.51)	16.2
(Not answered)	0.7

IF AGED 12 TO 15 OR IN FULL-TIME EDUCATION (CODE 1 AT Q.51)

54. Do you do a paid job of any sort at the moment - apart from anything you may do for your parents and get paid for?

	%
Yes	24.5
No	58.3
(Not answered)	0.3

55. What is the main place you go to for your full-time education?

	%
School	72.4
Sixth form college	4.0
College of Further Education	3.8
College of Higher Education/Tertiary College	0.5
University	1.4
Other (WRITE IN) ______	0.5
(Not answered)	0.5

56. Are you attending, or have you ever attended a fee-paying, private primary or secondary school in the United Kingdom?

	%
Yes	7.8
No	74.5
(Don't know)	0.3
(Not answered)	0.5

NOTE: "PRIVATE" INCLUDES INDEPENDENT/PUBLIC SCHOOLS, BUT EXCLUDES NURSERY SCHOOLS, VOLUNTARY-AIDED SCHOOLS AND "OPTED-OUT" GRANT-MAINTAINED SCHOOLS

57. **CODE AGE FROM Q.50:**

	%
Respondent aged 12 or 13	29.7
Respondent aged 14 to 19	53.5

n=580

CARD R

58a. Are you studying for any of the qualifications on this card?

	%
Yes	38.5
No	11.3
(Not answered)	3.6

IF YES AT a.

b. Which ones? Any others?
CODE ALL THAT APPLY

	%
GCSE / Scottish (SCE) **Ordinary** / Scottish (SLC) **lower grade** / Scottish (SUPE) **Ordinary**	27.6
GCE **'A' level/'S'** level / Scottish SCE/SLC/SUPE at **higher grade** / Scottish Certificate of Sixth Year Studies	9.5
GNVQ - **Foundation** / GNVQ - **Intermediate** / GNVQ - **Advanced** / **SCOTVEC** National Certificate modules	4.8
Overseas School Leaving Exam/Certificate	0.0

CARD S

59a. And are you studying for any of the qualifications on this card?

	%
Yes	6.2
No	44.5
(Not answered)	2.8

IF YES AT a.

b. Which ones? Any others?
CODE ALL THAT APPLY

	%
Recognised trade apprenticeship	-
RSA/other **clerical, commercial** qualification	0.5
City & Guilds Certificate - Craft/Intermediate/**Ordinary**/Part I	0.7
City & Guilds Certificate - **Advanced**/Final/Part II or Part III	0.2
City & Guilds Certificate - **Full technological**	0.2
BEC/TEC General/**Ordinary** National Certificate (ONC) or Diploma (OND)	1.9
BEC/TEC Higher/**Higher** National Certificate (HNC) or Diploma (HND)	0.3
Teacher training qualification	0.2
Nursing qualification	0.3
Other **technical or business** qualification/certificate	0.2
University or CNAA degree or diploma	1.6
Other recognised academic or vocational qualification	0.5

(WRITE IN) ____________

n=580

IF AGED 12-15 OR IN FULL-TIME EDUCATION

60. How old do you think you will be when you finish your full-time continuous education?

	%
16	11.4
17 or 18	22.8
19 or over	41.6
(Don't know)	6.8
(Not answered)	0.5

61a. And do you ever worry that you won't be able to get a job when you finish your education?

	%
Yes	57.4
No	23.3
(Don't know)	1.9
(Not answered)	0.5

IF YES AT a.

b. Is this ... **READ OUT** ...

	%
... a big worry,	11.1
a bit of a worry,	31.6
or just an occasional doubt?	14.5
(Don't know)	0.2

IF NOT IN FULL-TIME EDUCATION (CODE 2 AT Q.53)

62. What was the last place you went to for full-time education?

	%
School	10.5
Sixth form college	1.9
College of Further Education	3.3
College of Higher Education/Tertiary College	-
University	-
Other (WRITE IN) ____________	0.3
(Not answered)	0.2

63. Have you ever attended a fee-paying, <u>private</u> primary or secondary school in the United Kingdom?

	%,
Yes	0.5
No	15.6
(Don't know)	-

NOTE: "PRIVATE" INCLUDES INDEPENDENT/PUBLIC SCHOOLS, BUT EXCLUDES NURSERY SCHOOLS, VOLUNTARY-AIDED SCHOOLS AND "OPTED-OUT" GRANT-MAINTAINED SCHOOLS

64. How old were you when you left full-time continuous education?

	%
(Before 15)	0.2
15 or 16	10.3
17 or 18	5.5
19	0.2

ONLY

ONLY

OFFICE USE ONLY

n=580

65. And how likely is it that you will go back into full-time education within the next two years?
Is it ... READ OUT...

	%
... very likely,	1.7
fairly likely,	3.1
not very likely,	3.4
or not likely at all?	7.4
(Don't know)	0.5

ALL

66. **CODE AGE OF RESPONDENT FROM Q.50**

	%
Respondent aged 12 to 15 (code 1)	59.9
Respondent aged 16 to 19 (code 2)	39.5
(Not answered)	0.7

ALL AGED 16 TO 19
CARD T

67a. Have you passed any of the examinations on this card?
IF NOT: PROBE "Are you waiting to hear about about the results of any of these examinations?"

	%
Yes	26.5
No	7.8
Waiting to hear results	4.1
(Not answered)	1.0

IF YES AT a.

b. Which ones? Any others?
CODE ALL THAT APPLY

	%
GCSE - D-G **GCSE** - A-C Scottish (SCE) **Ordinary** Scottish (SLC) **lower grade** Scottish (SUPE) **Ordinary**	26.2
GCE **'A' level/'S'** level Scottish SCE/SLC/SUPE at **higher grade** Scottish Certificate of Sixth Year Studies	3.6
GNVQ - **Foundation** GNVQ - **Intermediate** GNVQ - **Advanced** **SCOTVEC** National Certificate modules	2.7
Overseas School Leaving Exam/Certificate	0.2

CARD U

68a. And have you passed any of the qualifications on this card?
IF NO: PROBE "Are you waiting to hear about the results of any of these examinations?"

	%
Yes	7.9
No, no taken/not passed	30.3
No, but taken and waiting to hear results	1.2

OFFICE USE ONLY

n=580

IF YES AT a.

68b. Which ones? Any others?
CODE ALL THAT APPLY

	%
Recognised trade apprenticeship completed	-
RSA/other **clerical, commercial** qualification	4.3
City & Guilds Certificate - Craft/Intermediate/**Ordinary**/Part I	1.7
City & Guilds Certificate - **Advanced**/Final/Part II or Part III	1.4
City & Guilds Certificate - **Full technological**	0.5
BEC/TEC General/**Ordinary** National Certificate (**ONC**) or Diploma (**OND**)	1.2
BEC/TEC Higher/**Higher** National Certificate (**HNC**) or Diploma (**HND**)	0.2
Teacher training qualification	-
Nursing qualification	-
Other **technical or business** qualification/certificate	0.3
University or CNAA degree or diploma	-
Other recognised academic or vocational qualification	0.7

(WRITE IN) ______________________

ASK ALL
CARD V

69a. Which, if any, of the things on this card would you say is your main ambition in life? Please read through the whole list before deciding.
CODE ONE IN COLUMN a.

b. And if you had to choose another ambition, which would it be?
CODE ONE IN COLUMN b.

	a. Main ambition	b. Next ambition
	%	%
To be happy	43.6	15.2
To be well off	8.3	9.3
To have good health	6.2	18.1
To have a good job	11.6	10.1
To be successful at work	9.4	10.8
To have my own home	1.0	6.3
To have a family	9.0	18.1
To travel and see the world	8.4	9.0
Something else (WRITE IN) ______	1.4	1.6
(None of these)	-	0.3
(Not answered)	1.0	1.2

70. Finally, a few questions about you and the people in your household. Including yourself, how many people live here regularly as members of this household?
CHECK INTERVIEWER MANUAL FOR DEFINITION OF HOUSEHOLD, IF NECESSARY.

MEDIAN:	4
(Not answered)	0.5%

ONLY

71. FOR EACH HOUSEHOLD MEMBER, CODE HIS OR HER RELATIONSHIP TO RESPONDENT

	PERSON NUMBER								
	2	3	4	5	6	7	8	9	10
	%	%	%	%	%	%	%	%	%
Mother	67.9	18.0	0.3	-	-	-	-	-	-
Father	21.0	48.3	0.3	-	-	-	-	-	-
Stepmother	0.5	0.7	0.5	-	-	-	-	-	-
Stepfather	0.2	3.5	0.2	-	-	-	-	-	-
(Step)brother/sister	1.0	15.5	63.7	28.5	11.2	2.9	0.5	-	-
Husband/wife/partner	1.2	-	-	-	-	-	-	-	-
(Step) child	0.3	1.2	0.3	0.3	-	-	-	-	-
Other relative	0.3	0.9	2.6	1.4	0.7	0.9	0.3	0.3	0.3
Not related	2.6	2.1	1.7	1.4	1.0	0.7	0.3	-	-

72. THANK RESPONDENT FOR HIS OR HER HELP AND COMPLETE Q.73 TO Q.74d

73. RECORD WHETHER ANYONE ELSE PRESENT DURING INTERVIEW

	%
Yes, throughout	35.0
Yes, sometimes	22.4
No	40.6
(Not answered)	2.0

74a. TIME INTERVIEW ENDED: 24 hour clock [ ][ ] : [ ][ ]

b. Total length of interview:
(see front cover and a. above)

MEDIAN: 30
(Not answered) 1.4

c. INTERVIEWER SIGNATURE

d. DATE OF INTERVIEW: DAY [ ][ ] MONTH [ ][ ] YEAR [9][4]

- PLEASE MAKE SURE THAT THE ARF (AND ANY CONTACT SHEET) IS COMPLETELY FILLED IN, INCLUDING THE RESPONDENT'S PERSON NUMBER AND FIRST NAME IN THE GRID ON PAGE 6 OF THE ARF.
- RETURN THE COMPLETED ARF (AND CONTACT SHEET, IF THERE IS ONE) TO THE FIELD OFFICE IN A SEPARATE ENVELOPE, NOT WITH THE QUESTIONNAIRE.
- CHECK THE QUESTIONNAIRE.
- DOUBLE CHECK THAT YOU HAVE FILLED IN ALL THE IDENTIFICATION NUMBERS, ESPECIALLY THE SERIAL NUMBER AND YOUR INTERVIEWER NUMBER ON THIS QUESTIONNAIRE.
- THEN RETURN THE QUESTIONNAIRE TO THE FIELD OFFICE AS SOON AS YOU CAN.

Index

Index entries refer to young people, unless otherwise specified. Tables are indicated by tab, but are not listed if there is also relevant text on the same page.

R

S